The Achievement of
Arthur Miller
New Essays

The Achievement of
Arthur Miller
New Essays

edited by
Steven R. Centola

Contemporary Research Press
Dallas / 1995

Library of Congress Cataloguing in Publication Data

The achievement of Arthur Miller : new essays / edited by Steven
R. Centola. -- 1st ed.
  p.   cm.
  Includes bibliographical references and index
  ISBN 0-935061-75-4 (cloth)
  1. Miller, Arthur, 1915- --Criticism and interpretation.
I. Centola, Steven.
PS3525.I5156Z512 1995
812'.52--dc20   95-34103

ISBN 0-935061-75-4

Contemporary Research Press
P.O. Box 7240
Dallas, Texas 75209

Printed in the United States of America

Contents

Introduction

The essays collected for this volume celebrate the accomplishments of America's greatest living playwright: Arthur Miller. Although Miller is universally regarded as one of this century's most distinguished playwrights, his reputation in America rests almost exclusively on the fame that came with commercial success very early in his career. Troubled by the poor reception that Miller's later work has received at the hands of his critics, many of the scholars contributing to this volume offer new interpretations of Miller's most severely undervalued plays. Others approach his master-works, *Death of a Salesman* and *The Crucible*, from new angles or give fresh treatment to such familiar subjects as Miller's tragic vision. A few also provide new insights into the linkage between thematic interests found in Miller's unpublished manuscripts and motifs—such as father-son relation-ships and questions pertaining to lost innocence and acceptance of personal responsibility—that surface repeatedly in his mature drama. Taken as a whole, then, the essays selected for this volume represent significant new perspectives of Miller's drama that reassess both his stature in the theater and the critical response to his later plays.

Even his detractors would probably agree that the time has come for a reappraisal of the body of work created by Miller. For nearly half of a century, Miller has been regarded as one of the two most important American playwrights to come out of the post-World War II era. Whenever the question is raised as to which twentieth-century American playwrights will be remembered for their artistic achievements, Miller's name almost always appears alongside that of Tennessee Williams. They are the two who best met the challenge handed down to them from Eugene O'Neill to keep America center stage in the world theater. What has been most unfortunate for Miller, however, is that for most of the American public and for all too many students of American drama, Miller's reputation rests solely on two plays created very early in his career: the classics *Death of a Salesman* (1949) and *The Crucible* (1953).

While there have literally been thousands of productions of Miller's plays around the world, in New York—the home of the American theater and the place where a playwright's fortune is either made or lost, Miller has suffered one setback after another throughout most of his career. Broadway productions of his new plays during the past three decades have generally not met with either much critical or commercial success. *After the Fall* provoked blistering tirades from critics in 1964; *The Creation of the World and Other Business* was quickly dismissed in 1972; *The American Clock* closed after only twelve performances in 1980; and neither *Danger: Memory!*, in 1987, nor *The Last Yankee*, in 1993, won rave reviews from the New York papers. Even *Broken Glass* received mixed reviews when it opened at the Booth Theater in April, 1994. *The Archbishop's Ceiling* never even made it to New York after its unsuccessful premiere in Washington, D.C., in 1977. The same fate awaited *Elegy for a Lady* and *Some Kind of Love Story* after the twin bill received bad reviews during the 1982 run at the Long Wharf Theater in New Haven, Connecticut.

During this same period of time, only revivals of Miller's earlier drama have opened to receptive audiences in New York. Ironically, the successful productions of such early works as *A View from the Bridge* in 1983, *Death of a Salesman* in 1984, and *All My Sons* in 1987 are primarily responsible for Miller's continued image as an icon in the American theater. Yet while being celebrated for plays created early in his career, Miller has seen virtually every new play he has created during the last two decades ignored in the States despite the fact that the same body of work has enjoyed great success abroad. Such indifference at home to his continued experimentation in the theater has justifiably angered the playwright. His dissatisfaction with the New York theater reached such a fevered pitch in 1991 that he decided to break with past tradition by staging a new play, *The Ride Down Mount Morgan*, outside the United States for its premiere. By opening this play in London—a first in the production history of his work, Miller felt he could strongly and visibly protest what he calls the "totally market-oriented"[1] theater in America.

What makes Miller's gesture of protest even more significant is the fact that he chose London as the site of the new production. Miller's plays have always enjoyed remarkable success in Great Britain. Annoyed with critics in his homeland who either have failed to understand his later plays or have constantly measured this body of work against his early successes, Miller has found in Europe the sympathetic response to his work that has long been absent in the States. In fact, audiences abroad not only appreciate his later dramas, but generally seem to prefer them to his early classics. This disparity in the European and American reactions to Miller's drama in recent years has given rise to the critical discussion that is provided in this volume.

The first essay in this volume addresses the problem of Miller's declining popularity in his native land and offers compelling explanations of the reasons for Miller's tremendous success abroad. Christopher Bigsby contends that Miller is more at home with European audiences because they do not believe that lost innocence is recoverable. Miller's tragic vision is compatible with the perspective of Europeans who accept human imperfection and recognize the need to offset it with responsible social action. In his homeland, Bigsby argues, Miller's tragic vision of the human condition collides with the American dream of strictly individual attainment.

Centering his discussion on stylistic features rather than thematic interests, Matthew Roudané considers a matter that has been largely ignored in Miller studies: the significance of didascalia in Miller's plays. Roudané analyzes the complex series of performative signals located within the stage directions which give rise to live spectacle, scenography, and directorial choice in Miller's plays. Because of the pronounced influence of Miller's didascalia, Roudané contends that within the stage directions to his plays lies much of Miller's theatrical power.

A more familiar subject in Miller's plays—the father-son relationship—is given a new twist by James Robinson. He considers the relationship between Miller's treatment of this motif in his apprentice play, *They Too Arise*, and his continued development of the theme in his later drama. What distinguishes Robinson's interpretation, however, is his contention that an examination of the unpublished apprentice play sheds light not only on Miller's treatment of the struggles between fatherhood and brotherhood in his later plays, but also on Miller's own desired but incomplete assimilation into mainstream American culture.

Also relying on unpublished manuscripts for her insights into Miller's development as an artist, Brenda Murphy takes a radical departure from previous studies of *Death of a Salesman* by discussing the transformation of Biff Loman's character from the pre-production scripts to the published stage version. Maintaining that the reformation of Biff Loman was essential to Miller's thematic purpose, Murphy argues that, while Biff's attainment of self-realization sufficiently counteracts the success myth and Willy's disaster, the revisions needed to set up Biff's revelation scene sacrifice the dramatic power and emotional intensity achieved in the earlier versions.

Death of a Salesman is also the subject of Janet Balakian's discussion. Viewing the public and private conflict in *Death of a Salesman* as inextricably linked, Balakian explains how Willy Loman's mental breakdown discloses the collapse of an American myth. Miller's expressionistic rendering of the drama inside Willy Loman's consciousness, says Balakian, confirms the overpowering impact of social laws on the individual psyche.

Grounding her discussion in feminist theories, Charlotte Canning also offers a provocative reading of *Death of a Salesman*. Challenging traditional interpretations of the female characters as ancillary to the main action in *Death of a Salesman*, Canning argues that women play a crucial role in almost every scene in Miller's most celebrated play. The women are not marginalized figures, says Canning, but are central to the play's development of character and conflict.

Arguably the most controversial reading of *Death of a Salesman* in this volume is offered, however, by Paula Langteau. Taking issue with the conventional view that *Death of a Salesman* is a document of social realism, Langteau presents her case for viewing the play as an early example of absurdist drama. Drawing upon Martin Esslin's seminal study of the Theatre of the Absurd, Langteau identifies several features of absurdist drama found in *Death of a Salesman*. Recognition of these features in Miller's drama, argues Langteau, aids in our understanding of Miller's technical achievements and thematic concerns.

Miller's other famous play, *The Crucible*, is discussed by Milton scholar Timothy Miller. Miller credits the playwright with understanding and accurately portraying seventeenth-century attitudes toward individual conscience and institutional authority. Through his act of civil and religious disobedience, John Proctor proves himself to be a Christian revolutionary. His rebellion, Miller asserts, derives from the strength of his faith and spiritual principles.

Approaching Miller's plays from a philosophical perspective, Qun Wang sets out to prove that Miller's drama is not designed to accentuate the relativity of truth but to challenge the validity of his characters' perception and commitment. Centering his discussion on *All My Sons, Death of a Salesman*, and *The Price*, Wang shows how tragedy derives from the ethical bewilderment that results when Miller's characters embrace values that betray their true interests in life.

Also using philosophy to underpin her discussion of Miller's tragic vision, Jeanne Johnsey associates the tragic moment in Miller's plays with the moment of consciousness described by Camus in his interpretation of the myth of Sisyphus. In *Death of a Salesman, The Crucible*, and *Playing for Time*, says Johnsey, the tragic moment occurs when the individual, in response to overwhelming external powers, reaches a moment of intense self-consciousness through insistence upon self-nomination. This transformative moment produces self-empowerment for the individual who temporarily experiences the nominative act and self as one.

A different perspective of Miller's tragic vision is offered by Terry Otten. Viewing the Fall as a central motif in Miller's canon, Otten shows how Miller adapts the Fall myth to portray the corruption of values in American society. Whereas all of Miller's plays point out the need for the acceptance of personal culpability, ironically, it is the temptation of innocence that poses the greatest threat to Miller's protagonists. Otten demonstrates that, in Miller's plays, it is the false claim of innocence that produces a self-ignorance which has tragic implications.

The remaining essays deal with the more recent, and most grossly undervalued, work by Miller. Robert A. Martin discusses the critical context of Miller's most controversial play, *After the Fall*, and indicts its detractors for failing to do justice to the work's universal themes and significant theatrical innovations. Either unable or unwilling to recognize Miller's real achievements in the play, the critics turned the public's attention to the autobiographical surface. In doing that, argues Martin, the critics failed themselves, their readers, and the play.

Another of Miller's underrated plays, *The American Clock*, is the subject of Gerald Weales's essay. Chronicling the rather unusual production history of the play, Weales explains how Miller successfully transforms the early unsuccessful version of *The American Clock* into an entertaining mural-mosaic-vaudeville. The spirit that informs the final stage version, as well as the decade it depicts, says Weales, is one of fun and frivolity tempered in hardship.

Isolating the philosophical underpinning that serves as a foundation for all of Miller's work, Steven R. Centola associates the two one-act plays contained in *Danger: Memory!* with both Miller's earlier drama and Jean-Paul Sartre's theater of situations. Even in his most recent drama, Miller reveals his continued interest in themes dealing with the acceptance of individual freedom and social responsibility. Through a Sartrean reading of *Clara* and *I Can't Remember Anything*, Centola shows that, even while demonstrating the awesome power of illusion and self-delusion, Miller's plays embody a moral code that celebrates self-determinism and the possibility to live an authentic existence.

But how can authenticity be achieved when the nature of reality is so indeterminate? This question, which underlies so much of Miller's later drama, gives rise to the central conflict in *The Ride Down Mount Morgan*, the subject of the last piece in this volume by June Schlueter. Schlueter's essay praises Miller's skill in depicting the elusive nature of the real in this fairly recent full-length drama. According to Schlueter, Miller deftly blurs the boundaries separating actual, remembered, and imagined events in the play to create a tantalizing ambiguity that dramatically reinforces his play's central theme. In the end, says Schlueter, we are left with an unfinished portrait of a life needing verification but trapped within the shifting contours of a problematic reality.

While the critical perspectives contained in this volume are offered in the hope of adding new insights into Miller's work, they in no way should be construed as an attempt to have the final word about Miller's art. There can be no final statement about Miller's drama. Like any great work of literature, Miller's plays ultimately defy formulaic postulations or reductive interpretations. Even the most cogent and comprehensive analysis of his work can never do justice to his artistic achievements. Miller's contributions to the world theater will almost certainly continue for years to come to be regarded as having lasting significance and enduring value. This new collection of critical perspectives of Arthur Miller's plays will hopefully entice others to take part in the never-ending conversation that discusses the literary and theatrical accomplishments of one of America's greatest playwrights.

Note

[1] Arthur Miller, as quoted in Matt Wolf, "An Exile of Sorts Finds a Welcome," *New York Times*, 13 October 1991, p. H6.

A British View of an American Playwright

Christopher W.E. Bigsby

If you were to turn to *The Oxford Companion to American Theatre*, this is what you would read about Arthur Miller: "Miller was a firmly committed leftist, whose political philosophizing sometimes got the better of his dramaturgy." And note the tense—*was*. His career apparently began with a play called *The Man Who Had All The Luck* which is "the story of a man who attributed his success to hard work." It would be difficult to imagine a description much wider of the mark than that since, as its title perhaps indicates, this is very precisely the opposite of the truth. Unsurprisingly, it is about a man who attributes his success to luck. But if you think that is bizarre, try this description of *Death of a Salesman*: a play "centering on the degeneration and suicide of an aging commercial traveller." That might be said, somewhat charitably, to miss some of the subtleties of the play.

Well, we can easily dismiss such an aberrant view, can't we? We could if it *were* quite so aberrant but, as I'll suggest in a moment, it isn't.

But, then, who cares about critics? This is the *theatre* we're talking about. What matters is production. A new play by Miller always makes a stir, does it not? Well, no, not entirely. *Death of a Salesman* certainly ran for 742 performances and won a Pulitzer Prize, but that was the last Pulitzer Miller has received to date—no prizes being awarded in the year he produced *After the Fall* or his most successful 60s play, *The Price*. Following the 742 performances of *Death of a Salesman* came *An Enemy of the People* with 36, *The Crucible* with 197 and *A View from the Bridge* with 149. *After the Fall* ran for 59 performances, *Incident at Vichy* 99, *The Creation of the World and Other Business* 20, *The Archbishop's Ceiling* 30, *The American Clock* 12. *Two-Way Mirror* (then called *Two by AM*) didn't make it beyond New Haven while the new lease of life for *The Archbishop's Ceiling*, *Two-Way Mirror* and the early play *The Man Who Had All The Luck* depended on a British publisher.

In an interview published in *American Theatre* in May, 1987, Robert Brustein, who once described O'Neill as a "charter member of a cult of inarticulacy," denounced Tennessee Williams for dragging a Southern segregationalist into the middle of a sexual nightmare in *Sweet Bird of Youth*, and denounced Miller for addressing the question of McCarthyism in *The Crucible* through "an obfuscating treatment of the Salem witch trials," complained of American playwrighting from the 1930s to the 1960s, and particularly of the work of Odets, Williams and Miller, that it was "all preplanned, therefore predictable." Cause A inevitably led to Effect B, adding that, "I think we've been more and more discovering that that's not the way the universe happens." In other words Miller was being accused not simply of creating plays at odds with Brustein's sense of dramaturgy; he was actually out of step with the universe. Brustein, Professor of Drama at Yale and then Harvard, continued: "It seems odd to say this but there was a time when progressive, optimistic views of the world totally dominated our literature, particularly our drama. It made our drama a travesty." It's hard to know what to make of such a comment. The most charitable explanation would seem to be that his advocacy of Samuel Beckett, on the one hand, and the experiments of the American avant-garde, on the other, required him to attack what he saw as opposing forms of drama as well as apparently opposing interpretations of the real. But what interests me is the extent to which his reading of Williams and Miller is so inadequate. Not merely, writing in 1987, does he seem to ignore their later work, which could scarcely be said to match his model—works such as Tennessee Williams's *Outcry* and *Red Devil Battery Sign* or Miller's *The Archbishop's Ceiling* and *Two-Way Mirror*—but he chooses to interpret their earlier plays in terms which do little to explain or to explore their particular qualities.

But Brustein was not alone. Three years earlier, in *Performing Arts Journal*, the playwright Mac Wellman suggested that "most of O'Neill and Arthur Miller has come to resemble a collection of yammering skeletons," because they fail to acknowledge "the despair of ninety-five per cent of the population" and because their characters are "made up of explanations, aggregations of explicated motives, explicated past behaviour, wholly knowable and wholly contrived." Such playwrights, he suggested, are in thrall to naturalism and incapable of approaching the greatness of Beckett. His own preferred American playwright is Len Jenkin who, interestingly, is himself rather more generous in his response to other writers and styles, looking for a sense of wonder which can be found, he suggests, in everything from the realistic to the sublimely outrageous and which has to be there, "in the text and through and through." For Mac Wellman Miller is a simple naturalist for whom character is merely an aggregation of incident and psychological trauma, what O'Neill was fond of calling "holding the family Kodak up to ill nature."

On the one hand this ignores the subversive quality of naturalism, so often concerned with the disintegration of character and the disruption of causality by contingency, the space between desire and fulfillment. On the other it ignores the degree to which that naturalism is itself disrupted by Miller, most obviously in the later plays but also in *Death of a Salesman, A View from the Bridge* and *After the Fall.*

It is not difficult, of course, to see the nonsense of these remarks by Brustein and Mac Wellman in relation to these plays, but what of *All My Sons,* a work which I suspect probably inspired them and led to these facile generalizations?

All My Sons is a well-made play. One of the ironies of criticism is that that is a pejorative description, pejorative because it is intended to imply that its meanings are exhausted in the telling, they leave no residue, that no incident exists which does not render up its significance, no word is spoken which will not eventually be seen as subscribing to a model of experience in which there is no redundancy. The very coherence of the text implies the coherence of the world which it describes. The set, it is presumed, is resolutely realistic. Everything fits.

Arthur Miller, as is by now probably well known, is a carpenter. He made the bed in which he sleeps, the desk at which he works, the table from which he eats his meals. *All My Sons,* it is suggested, is just another table, perfectly constructed, fully functional, every joint sliding precisely into place with none of those rough edges which make theatre disturbing. Speaking out of a 1960s experimental theatre, in which the writer was seen as authoritarian and language as a distraction from the visceral power of a theatre rediscovering its physicality, this kind of drama seemed obsolete. Speaking out of a 1980s experimental theatre, in which the consciousness of the audience became a primary focus and in which the audience was required to fill spaces deliberately left blank by writer or director, the well-made play seemed to close doors rather than open them. Nora's slamming door in *A Doll's House* seemed emblematic. And, indeed, it was none too clear whether Brustein's strictures should be seen as applying equally to Chekhov, Ibsen and Strindberg who might also be thought to fall foul of inhabiting altogether the wrong universe. But they perhaps had the virtue of being untainted with optimism.

There is no smooth theatre unless some director should choose to sandblast it or an actor merely to impersonate another, for actors and directors transform what they touch. Theatre is a form of alchemy and if the end-product is not always gold at least certain transformations have been effected. Frederick March, Lee J. Cobb, Dustin Hoffman and Warren Mitchell have all played the part of Willy Loman in *Death of a Salesman.* They spoke the same lines to the same characters but they spoke them differently to different audiences, in different sets, in front of different people, in different theatres, at different times on different continents. As the Swedish director Igmar Bergman has said, the theatre is about repetition: always the same, only different. The theatre is about repetition and it is about change. Dustin Hoffman in the stage version of *Death of a Salesman* was not the same Willy Loman as he was in the television version. And what is true of actors is no less true of us. Whenever any of us open our mouths we speak the past. The words we use have passed through other mouths. They've been shaped, over time, by pleasures and pains not our own. They're like our own, but they're not our own. They've shed and accumulated meanings. Perhaps that's one reason we're drawn to the theatre. It enacts our own central dilemma, as actors inhabit someone else's words and struggle to make them their own, just as we try to imprint ourselves on the given.

To state the obvious, the production of *All My Sons* which played in London, at the Young Vic in 1992, was not the *All My Sons* in which Colin Blakely and Rosemary Harris starred at Wyndhams Theatre many years ago, nor was it the Royal Exchange Theatre, Manchester's production of which its director Gregory Hersov remarked, "What we see at the end of the play is Clytemnestra sobbing before the temple." Incidentally, Rosemary Harris, having played Kate Keller for nine months was still unsure at the end of that period just how much she, the character, knew or suspected of her husband's actions. Did Miller's hand perhaps slip so that the mortice and tenon didn't quite fit or is the play perhaps a little rougher, a little less well-made than it appears. She found the play disturbing to act, creating within her contradictory emotions which took her the best part of twelve hours to recover from after each performance. It's hard to believe that that didn't communicate to audiences. But what she found in the play is perhaps not what other Kates found when confronted with Joe Kellers who themselves assumed different levels of self-knowledge.

For Gregory Hersov the very interconnections which alarmed Brustein are the source of the play's strength. As he says, "the characters' destinies are fully written; there are not holes or evasions." His account of the play is of one which makes it a play for the 1980s and '90s, precise and timely:

> Joe Keller's crime in *All My Sons* is the modern riddle of our free market world. In the interests of our well-being, self-esteem, love for our family, business decisions are taken that destroy those very possibilities in other human beings, whom we never meet. One sunny day, in his own garden, Joe Keller finds out the awful truth of his actions. His whole family and neighbourhood are also brought face to face with his trouble. Their previously held ideas of themselves and their world are destroyed, their "connection" with everything discovered. The setting of the play, with its reassuring images coupled with its basic issues, connect directly with our modern existence.

So connection becomes a key issue, but connection perhaps implies a closed circle in which meaning is contained within the circle. But meaning spills out, is sometimes incomplete, and I'm sure that he would be the first to admit that this account only begins the process of understanding *All My Sons*. By no means everything is discovered, in the sense of resolved. For this is also a play about betrayal, about fathers and sons, about America, about self-deceit, about self-righteousness, about egotism presented as idealism, about a fear of mortality, about guilt, about domestic life as evasion, about the space between appearance and reality, about the suspect nature of language, about denial, about repression, about a kind of despair finessed into hope about money, about an existence resistant to our needs, about a wish for innocence when, as Miller was later to say in his autobiography, innocence kills, about a need for completion, about the gulf between the times we live in and the people we wish to believe ourselves to be, about the fragility of what we take to be reality, about time as enemy and time as moral force and so on. . . . As they used to say in language primers for foreign students, a table is a table. A table is not a play. A play is not a table.

Casually dismissed as a realist, in fact Miller has experimented with form, disassembled character, compressed and distended language, and seen in the theatrical plot a paradigm of other constructs having to do with identity and social form. His commitment to a morally accountable and socially responsible self has not inhibited him from exploring the contingency alike of character and public myths. That is clear in the late plays—*The Archbishop's Ceiling, Two-Way Mirror, The American Clock*, but also in the early ones. *Death of a Salesman* folds time so that past and present press upon one another in a play in which a disintegrating psyche is both subject and method. *The Crucible* is nothing less than a debate about the nature of the real. But in a fundamental way his theatre exists to bear witness to those human necessities which survive a knowledge of their fragility. The coercive fictions of the state or the self are nonetheless corrosive for their fictiveness and the theatre nonetheless real for its theatricality. It is that reality which Miller serves.

And what of the accusation that Miller fails to share that sense of despair that Mac Wellman insists ninety-five percent of the American population share, that "progressive, optimistic view of the world" which Brustein sees as so at odds with the way the universe operates? The irony, of course, is that like O'Neill before him Miller has always embraced a tragic view of life at odds with American myths of perfectibility. Indeed in his autobiography he identifies as a central theme of American writers a critique of the American dream with its faith in change, improvement, ameliorisation. Indeed it's arguable that it is his tragic sensibility which has in some senses created a gulf between himself and his American audience. O'Neill suspected as much in his own case. But tragedy and despair are not good bedfellows, and it is true that Miller sees despair as a dangerous virus. Like Bellow before him he sees the absurd as flirting with danger for in a world without values what distinguishes the concentration camp guard from his victim? And it is worth remembering that Bellow and Miller are both Jewish. As Miller has said, "Now all the European playwrights, and the rest of the writers, can tell me that it's hopeless, and by and large, it is, but it's not one hundred percent hopeless. That's all I'm about to tell you." It is not his refusal to embrace despair which potentially puts him at odds with his American public. It is, perhaps, his tragic sense of life—albeit a tragic sense of life invaded by and invested with a powerful sense of the tragic.

Why do the British take to the work of Arthur Miller? Perhaps because he's a writer who deals with words and ours is a culture which privileges language. And though his plays have an emotional power I think we recognize and sympathize with characters, like Joe Keller and Willy Loman, John Proctor and Eddie Carbone, who have difficulty expressing their own emotions. America is a culture in which the individual severed from his society is a culture hero, whether he is riding out of a western town or walking the mean streets, a culture in which the notion of an individual's responsibility for the welfare of those around him is treated with suspicion. In Britain, however, that notion is rooted deeply. Miller's view of human nature is that it is fundamentally flawed. In a society which pursues perfection, spiritual and sexual fulfillment, a society which once announced as its goal the pursuit of happiness, he stages the imperfect lives of imperfect individuals and sees in these personal failings the root of national and social failings. America doesn't want to be told that we live after the fall. President after president stands up to deliver his state of the union address and tells the citizenry that innocence is recoverable—that America is a city on the hill, a new Jerusalem, a thousand points of light. A new society is possible, a new deal, a new frontier and now a new order. Henry Ford's conviction that history is bunk is in a sense a national slogan. What Miller has said of the American writer could be applied more generally to the American individual celebrated by American myths: "The tongue has been cut from the past, leaving him alone to begin from the beginning, from the Creation and the first naming of things seen for the first time." In Europe the past is not so easily laid in the grave. Even as we speak it is making its demands on the present across Eastern and Central Europe and Miller has never forgotten the lesson of the Depression or the camps. Maybe that's why the British respond to Miller as the French responded to William Faulkner when he was out of print in America. For him too the past is not the past. But Miller is not the first American writer to find a more enthusiastic audience abroad so that I am tempted to broaden this to a general principle. What place, after all, did America find for Edgar Allan Poe or for Herman Melville? Scott Fitzgerald died largely ignored, Nathaniel West wholly so. When he was awarded the Nobel Prize it was a rare bookstore that had copies of Faulkner's novels and when he won the same prize Isaac Bashevis Singer was still thought of as vaguely foreign ("Pole Wins Nobel," announced the *Los Angeles Times*). O'Neill died alienated, William Inge by suicide, bewildered by the peremptory judgement of a society which had picked him up and then tossed him aside. Tennessee Williams died as he feared he would, and as O'Neill had, alone in a hotel room. America has many more millionaires than people who could tell you the name of Arthur Miller's plays of the 1970s and 80s. The man who speaks a writer's lines has greater fame than the writer.

And America has always disregarded its drama in particular. There is still no comprehensive history of American drama. In the standard literary histories it is relegated to a footnote. Spiller, Thorpe, Canby, and Johnson devote just 56 of their 1442 pages to it (4%). In the 1980s the *Macmillan History of the Literature of the United States* gave 14 out of 204 pages to drama and the Harvard Guide 43 out of 606 pages, and this despite the fact that American drama has been the dominant drama of the 20th century.

The first critical study of Arthur Miller was published in Britain as was the first study of David Mamet; the first study of Edward Albee appeared in Belgium; one of the best critics of black drama is French. When O'Neill died he left production of his last great plays in the hands of a Swedish theatre and now Miller has chosen to open *The Last Yankee* in London.

David Mamet has said that American playwrights can only reach a certain level of fame. If they wanted to go any further they have to be promoted honorary Englishmen. Miller has been so promoted. In 1991 he chose to open his new play, *The Ride Down Mount Morgan*, in London's West End rather than in New York. It was a decision which reflected his dismay at the decline of a Broadway theatre which at that time, he insisted, was staging only one play with any serious pretensions, and that a Neil Simon comedy. But there were other reasons why Britain had become a more receptive environment for his drama. There were altogether practical reasons for turning to Britain.

To begin with, in Britain he is regarded as a living playwright rather than an object to be placed under glass in the Smithsonian as a relic of the 40s and 50s. We know, as on the whole America does not, the late plays. Our finest companies have produced them. Indeed Miller himself has reminded us that,

> it's difficult to find actors who will stay with a play for more than a few months because actors are off to the movies and television and the play requires mature actors. There is still a tradition in England. We don't have that any more. Our

> theatre is a stepping stone to the movies. Beyond the tyranny of the *New York Times* the people who come now are basically interested in seeing a personal appearance of the star. When the playwrights are not the main attraction the theatre is in decline. The theatre is a tribune of the people—but no longer.

In effect he had been driven from the public stage from the mid-1950s to the mid-1960s. Political reaction meant that there was no longer an audience for a playwright dedicated to testing American values. When he returned, the theatre itself had changed. The sixties saw a revolt against the playwright and against language itself. Artaud-influenced theatre groups chose to privilege the actor and to treat with some suspicion those distinguishing marks of a Miller play: rationality, lucidity and the sequential logic of morality. Theirs was a theatre in which the body was legitimized and the Reality Principle subordinated to the Pleasure Principle. This was never true in Britain, where for cultural, class and educational reasons, language remained central and physicality was distrusted. Miller's theatre, resolutely committed to the word, was readily embraced.

Later, the academic critic—the deconstructionist and the feminist—saw little reason to respond to Miller. Those like Paul De Mann—dismissive of history, perhaps for their own reason, were hardly likely to respond to a writer for whom it was vital, an aspect of moral continuity which could not be denied. Those dismissive of the self were perhaps likely to treat with suspicion a writer whose characters were forever shouting their names into the wind—"I'm Joe Keller"; "I'm Willy Loman"; "I'm Eddie Carbone"; "I'm John Proctor still—and there's the wonder of it." Those looking for drama which places women at the centre were likely to be suspicious of Miller—more especially if they knew nothing of *After the Fall, Playing for Time* or *Two-Way Mirror*.

Then again, Miller has always been concerned with the flawed self, the tragic sensibility, and this in a culture whose central myths have to do with innocence, optimism and perfectibility. Europe has quite other myths and a history which offers a different vision of human nature, one which finds in Miller's serious engagement with moral issues, as in his increasing fascination with the nature of the real and the substance of identity, a writer of genuine power and fascination. In the seventies and eighties when much (though not all) American theatre, reflecting changes in the culture, had turned towards privatism, Miller remained committed to an exploration of social issues in a way which found a response in Britain whose theatre had, since the fifties, been socially oriented and in a continent in which notions of private guilt and social responsibility had a clear historical referent. Perhaps not only because of his admiration for Greek drama and the work of Ibsen, but also because of his Jewish background, Miller has always insisted on the reality of the *polis*, the notion that the individual is ineluctably part of the social system and derives his or her identity from interaction with others. From this derives a moral responsibility. This truth, however, he offers in a culture profoundly suspicious of social systems. Nixon's and Reagan's America, which forms the setting for *The Ride Down Mount Morgan*, seemed to many to be based on a denial of the social contract and a legitimizing of a self detached from personal and public responsibility.

The Ride Down Mount Morgan is a play about a man with no morals but, at least in his own mind, complete integrity. Lyman Felt is a bigamist who has convinced himself that, as a result, he has given two women what they wanted, bearing the burden of knowledge himself. One night, returning to one of them down a snow-covered mountainside, having removed a warning barrier, he crashes and ends up in a hospital bed where the two wives come together, though whether in his mind or in actuality is never conclusively established. If Miller's drama is based on what happens when one of his characters can no longer walk away then Lyman's circumstances, immobilized in a plaster cast, ensure that he must now confront his situation. In Miller's words, he "falls into his life," a man who has "a limitless capacity for self-deception and for integrity." Like our civilization, he has said, Lyman "is capable of enormous construction and destruction."

The play has ironic echoes of *Death of a Salesman*. In the earlier play a man called Loman had tried to claim the American dream, reaching for success in material and sexual terms, only to find himself with nothing. In *The Ride Down Mount Morgan* a man called Lyman appears to have everything, money and sexual possessions, but now has to confront himself. In the earlier play a shadowy figure called Uncle Ben warns against fighting fair with strangers. In this one a similarly shadowy figure—Lyman's dead father—warns him not to trust or forgive. Lyman is part poet, part business-man, a division equally apparent in *Death of a Salesman*, though there, as in *The Price*, these qualities were divided between two brothers, almost as though they were enacting a schism at the heart of the American experience, a culture born out of a spiritual and material impulse. The themes, so apparent in all his plays—guilt, betrayal—are at the centre of this play, too. Even the structure of *The Ride Down Mount Morgan* resembles that of *Death of a Salesman*, *After the Fall*, and *Timebends*, as time is collapsed and events are summoned into existence by a mind in which memory and desire are merely two witnesses brought before a court in which the audience alone constitutes the jury.

For all that, this is a play which speaks out of its own moment even as it speaks to others. Written in the seventies and eighties it has elements of both decades, an original reference to Nixon's election being replaced in the course of rehearsals by one to Reagan's. Thus, Lyman voices both the 1970s slogan, "believe in your feelings," and a 1980s cynicism: "We're all ego plus an occasional prayer." As Miller has remarked of Lyman,

> he's the quintessential Eighties Man, the man who has everything, but there's no end to his appetite. He keeps saying he's telling the truth about himself, but in fact he's had to conceal everything . . . he discovers that betrayal is the first law of life, that you can either be loyal to yourself or to others but not to both. Your only hope is to end up with the right regrets.

It is, Miller insists, "a completely political play." So, in a sense it is, but, for Miller, the political is of a piece with what he has called "the biology of morals." There is no politics not rooted in individual decisions, while private morality and public morality are of the same flesh. Lyman has collapsed his world into a privatism whose politics he chooses not to address. For Miller he is "the apotheosis of the individualist who has arrived at a point when the rest of the world has faded into insignificance."

As Miller has said, Lyman "has a lot of terrific qualities":

> He has an appetite for life. His is a Faustian character and like our civilization he is capable of enormous construction and destruction. He is intent on expressing himself and not suppressing his instinctual life, on living full in every possible way. That is his integrity and he will confront the worst about himself and proceed from it. The question is, "What about other people?" He believes that a man can be faithful to himself or to other people but not to both. This is the dilemma of the play. He manages to convince himself and I believe some part of the audience that this is a higher value than other people—the psychic survival of the individual. The play has no solution to this. If I did I could probably cure a lot of people—but it is laid out in front of us.

And is this *not* a playwright for today?

Lyman wishes to live without guilt and without unsatisfied longings. Convinced that a man can be faithful to himself or to others but not to both and that the first law of life is betrayal, he sets out to follow the logic of his own desires, seeing this as a form of integrity. In doing so he exults in escaping definition, becoming one person with one wife and another with the other. Theodora, the older of the two, is deeply conservative in all things, tense, possessive; Leah is relaxed, considers abortion, lives life in the fast stream. In one sense, though, they are literally what he makes of them; at others, what he fears or suspects.

The play's original chronology had Lyman at fifty-six years old, just a year short of the age at which his father died. That father's appearance, trailing a length of black cloth in which he offers to ensnare his son, is thus an expression of Lyman's mortality and an explanation, perhaps, for his desire to resist habit and definition alike. The shifted chronology hardly undermines this, though it does, perhaps, blunt its edge. For the fact is that by the end of the play he seems close to discovering some kind of meaning in the very banalities which he has fled, in the insignificant details of daily living and continuing relationships. In the meantime, though, he has sought in danger an antidote to routine, only to discover that there is a routine even to betrayal.

The Ride Down Mount Morgan poses director and actors with a major challenge. It is comic without being a comedy and tragic without being a tragedy. You might say that bigamy implies a touch of farce while adultery suggests a level of pain: those, at any rate, have been their theatrical connotations. Here, the humour slowly darkens toward irony. The actors have to shift from one mood to another. Lyman himself, who at times steps out and away from the plaster-encased figure on the bed, has both to be able to look down on himself with a sense of detachment and remain passionate about the women he purports to love and the life he wishes to redeem through action. As an audience we see partly through his eyes, his memory, which sometimes reproduces the past, sometimes stylizes it, and partly, or so it seems, independently of the man who has perhaps staged this drama out of his own sense of doubt and incompletion as out of his desire for the danger of crisis. Judgement is thus no easy matter.

Because of this double vision it is difficult, too, to make definitive judgements on the two women, for if they seem to represent, at times, too clear a polarity, this is in large degree because they are presented to us through the transforming imagination and memory of Lyman. The real is no more stable here than it had been in *Two-Way Mirror*, and yet, of course, since Lyman inhabits the world he invents and responds to the women he projects there is a reality to memory and to those constructions which he makes of those he encounters. Indeed from *The Golden Years* onwards Miller has been concerned to acknowledge the degree to which myths are no less real than the diminished world which inspires their creation.

The Ride Down Mount Morgan is a portrait of an imperial self, absorbing others, colonizing their lives. Staged at a time of other collapsing empires—this time public and political rather than private and psychological—it offers a diagnosis and perhaps even a prognosis of a culture itself appropriating moral rhetoric to disguise moral decay. Greed and self-righteousness co-exist. Sensuality is a temptation, an isolating appetite which leads to the breaking of personal contracts. In play after play that small fracture widens into a radical dislocation of social responsibilities. "Why are our betrayals what we remember?" asks Miller, "because those are the acts that bring the world down."

There is no resolution to *The Ride Down Mount Morgan*. If betrayal is indeed bred in the bone perhaps there could be none. There is, however, in the play's structuring device, a reminder that the past is never the past; it lives on into the present as evidence of the link between action and consequence and hence between will and moral being. And though such continuities may be the basis of ethical demands they are not suggestive of a static self. Lyman Felt is various. What he seeks is some constancy beneath his various selves. Like many of Miller's characters he wants to drag the world into alignment with his self-image. The world is no less resistant in his case than in that of Willy Loman and Eddie Carbone, but, where they die, he lives on. Possibility survives. Comedy asserts a restraining pressure on the tragic potential, a liberating force on the closed world which seals off the fate of many of his protagonists.

From 1968 onwards, with the production of *The Price*, comedy has played a more central role in Miller's work than in the early plays, touched with humour though they are. His own response is to suggest that with age "it gets funnier." Perhaps. There was always irony, born out of a gulf between reality and appearance. Now, though, his sense of the protean nature of identity and the insubstantiality of the real leaves him with moral certainties which can only be sustained with an awareness of their fragility. Late plays have a way of drifting in the direction of comedy, albeit for Miller, as for O'Neill before him, touched with a leaven of darkness. Comedy becomes value. So it does here. But then, so, too, does theatre itself. As Miller has indicated:

> Watching a play is not like lying on a psychiatrist's couch or sitting alone in front of the television. In the theatre you can sense the reaction of your fellow citizens along with your own reactions. You may learn something about yourself, but sharing it with others brings a certain relief—the feeling that you are not alone, you're part of the human race. I think that's what theatre is about and why it will never be finished.

It is certainly what Miller's theatre has been about and continues to be about, for to his mind it is an antidote to that very privatism, that concern with the self over others, which is the temptation offered to us all and which makes possible private and public betrayals.

For all his recognition of the relativity of truth, for all his acceptance that reality may be no more than a series of performed gestures, Miller is unwilling to let go of certain fixed points. The rocks beneath the waves are not figments of our imagination and the responsibility to indicate their presence remains. There are certain human necessities which must be acknowledged. It may no longer be possible to believe that below the mud is solid granite but, for Miller, beyond the fantasies, the self-deceptions, the distortions of private and public myths are certain obligations which cannot be denied. The present cannot be severed from the past nor the individual from his social context that, after all, is the basis of his dramatic method and of his moral faith. For if the chickens do not come home to roost we are no longer tied to our actions. A world without consequence is a world without meaning and to a writer who began his career as an admirer of the Greek theatre such an assumption renders theatre itself null. What else is theatre, after all, than a shared apprehension of a common condition, an acknowledgement that there is a level at which the experience of one is the experience of all? It is that simple truth which lies at the heart of Arthur Miller's drama and which, outside of his writing, has led him to speak out in the face of investigative committees in his own country or the oppressed around the world. His real achievement, however, is as a writer whose plays have proved so responsive to the shifting pressure of the social world and whose characters embody that desperate desire for dignity and meaning which is the source of their wayward energy, their affecting irony and their baffled humanity. And to hell with Robert Brustein.

If the American theatre has become what Miller calls "a mendicant theatre" then there are still other theatres, for we are all anyway—in his telling phrase—"provinces of one great human empire now." There are places, even, where the *New York Times* and Robert Brustein do not prevail. One of these is to be found in a small off-shore island. As to why the British are more receptive, maybe it is for none of the reasons suggested. Maybe it is simply that at a time when British drama—and French, German and Italian—has not been particularly impressive we are reminded of the existence of a major writer across the Atlantic. Or maybe, who knows, the British respond to Arthur Miller for the very simplest of reasons. He writes outstanding plays. At the age of seventy-eight he still engages the moment. He writes about characters whose fate we are persuaded to care about and does so in plays which will live as long as people are prepared to come together, to sit in the presence of others, and to see on the stage actors who persuade us that we have a connection not only with one another but with all those who came before us and whose dilemmas we recognize as our own. After all, we are all their sons and daughters.

From Page to Stage:
Subtextual Dimensions in the Theater of Arthur Miller

Matthew C. Roudané

Arthur Miller privileges language. While acknowledging aesthetic distinctions concerning the status of language in cinematic texts and playtexts, Miller suggests in the "Preface" to his 1990 screenplay *Everybody Wins* that "the word made flesh may *be* more and suggest less. It [the writer's job] is a very mysterious business, and by no means a simple question of better or worse, but of differences of aesthetic feeling, of timbre and tissue, that accompany differences of form."[1] The "differences" to which Miller alludes raise important questions about the playwright's theory of art and, indeed, the creative process itself. Above all, Miller inscribes "differences" of dramatic representation through language, a language "made flesh" when Mildred Dunnock and Lee J. Cobb first filled the stage with word and body at the Morosco Theater on February 10, 1949, during *Death of a Salesman*. Ever concerned with linguistic transferences from page to stage, Miller views the word as image, and image as the visible means to performance grace. Such a belief in the efficacy of his language enables Miller--when he is at his best--to elevate his dialogues of cliche to original poetry, an issue that he himself has pondered throughout his career. "Words, unable to imitate reality," Miller reflects, "must in their nature serve it up in metaphoric guise. . ." (*Everybody Wins*, p. v).

Thus, ever since Miller reinvented the American stage with *Death of a Salesman*, theatergoers have been dazzled by the playwright's dialogue and the way in which language animates his stage. All serious scholars of his theater, from Robert A. Martin and Gerald Weales to June Schlueter and C.W.E. Bigsby, note that Miller conflates the text/performance dialectic through a language that, paradoxically, appears as banal as it is eloquent. Miller's informal syntax, his characters' platitudes, their hyperbole, however, quickly transcend the cliched, and we now have long recognized the playwright's lexical inventiveness. In plays like *The Price* and *Incident at Vichy*, Miller's idiolect defines character and characterization; in a play like *After the Fall*, his language extends, however slightly, the ontological status of theatricality itself, its ritualized texture revealing the interiority of each character's consciousness. In both text and performance, Miller's plays engage audiences on multiple levels: visually, a performance of *Salesman* in certain scenes becomes a tantalizing display of the carnivalesque, the acting of the Lomans problematizing the truth/illusion matrix (especially when Miller bends time in the flashback scenes); theatrically, a performance of *After the Fall* decenters audiences with its shifting of a character's consciousness and the audiences' perceptions of Quentin's and Maggie's stage and staged action. In context of philosophic intellection, *The Crucible* invites a kind of metaphysical speculation that we have come to enjoy in Shakespeare's *King Lear* or Beckett's *Waiting for Godot*. As a theatrician of the ethical, then, Miller stages plays about, as Herbert Blau would say, the watchers watching the watchers watch. But how does Miller stage what we watch? How does Miller move from mere text to a broader cultural context? Certainly one way to answer such questions is to examine his language, the most obvious element that moves a Miller performance from page to stage.

However, relatively little attention has been given to another language Miller privileges, a metalanguage that nearly rivals the overt dialogue of a play: the "didascalic discourse," or what is more commonly referred to as the stage directions. Although several critics--Roman Ingarden, Michael Issacharoff, and Patricia A. Suchy immediately come to mind--discuss the performative functions of the didascalia, few have attempted to define the major features of didascalia and the ways in which such didascalic structures affect matters of theatrical representation and, finally, our deeper understanding of Arthur Miller's theater.

I will begin with a theoretical account of the five major forms of didascalia, using selected scenes from Miller's plays to make the theoretic concrete, and will end with a discussion of the theatrical implications of Miller's extensive use of didascalia. I am less concerned with Miller's "sacred text" than with its borders: the implied action inscribed in the margins of the playtext. If what I say is true, we will see that within the didascalia--the marginalia of dramatic representation--lies much of Miller's theatrical power. Didascalic language, representation, and Miller's theater become a paradoxical mixture of theatrical discourses, for Miller literalizes a play through the language of the text, and yet in virtual performance, actors deliteralize that same text. Audiences never *see* the textualized version of stage notes (their invisibility in live performance precludes such vision), but clearly audiences *see* the traces, the representative effects of the stage notes as reified by an actor's particular frown or the intensity with which he or she delivers a word.

Didascalic discourse emerges as an integral part of a Miller play. Why? Because the playwright appropriates the didascalia to such an extent that to ignore them is to oversimplify a major (if subtextual) component of Miller's imaginative structures. Between the theory and practice of reading--and then staging of *Elegy for a Lady* or *The Archbishop's Ceiling*--lies a complex series of performative issues: how we read Miller's playscript and turn it into live spectacle, questions of authorial control and directorial choice, the increasingly problematic relationship of text and performance, theories of proxemics, scenography, the audience, and the like make a Miller play a multivocal and metalingual enterprise. Miller's spoken words and nonverbal gestures, combined with audience reception, culminate in what Michael Issacharoff and Robin F. Jones call a "performing text," and invite critics to explore "the dynamic relation between script and performance, performance and reception."[2] I would suggest that such a "dynamic relation" seems more pronounced because of the influence of Miller's subtext, the didascalia.

Toward a Typology of Didascalic Discourse

Before turning to selected Miller plays, it seems sensible to define some theoretical terms by constructing a typology of didascalia. These stage directions, or didascalia, are much more complex than scholars have acknowledged, for they range in scope and emphasis from the most simple-- "*exit Polonius*" or "*enter Claudius*"--to the most complex: the lengthy novelistic prefaces for which Shaw is renowned, for instance. Although using the term "didascalia" over "stage directions" may seem unnecessary, I think "didascalia" better captures the intellectual as well as emotional impact of these seemingly minor notations. We risk trivializing the rich performative functions embedded in didascalic discourse if we merely dismiss them, as John Searle does, as a mere "recipe for baking a cake." Marvin Carlson, by contrast, has recognized the significance of stage directions and discusses the five primary forms of didascalia.[3]

The Attributive Didascalia

The *attributive* didascalia, the most fundamental of all notations, identify the person speaking: who's speaking to whom. "This type of direction is so universal," Carlson observes, "that normally within itself it serves as a distinguishing feature of the dramatic mode." Despite the disregard of the didascalia by many actors and scholars, the attributive notations are "the most widely respected of the didascalic functions in performance" (p. 37). Carlson also points out that, "though lines are often cut, rewritten, or rearranged, their assignment to other fictive speakers is very rare, found most often in experimental interpretations so far from the original that they are usually considered adaptations" (p. 43). Thus in *Incident at Vichy* we find the following attributive didascalia: "BAYARD--*he looks at Von Berg for a moment, then addresses all*: 'I don't understand it, but take my advice.'"[4] Or in *The Price* we read: "ESTHER: 'I'll go to the cleaner, dear. I'll be back soon.' *With a step toward the door--to Solomon*: 'Will you be very long?'"[5] Obviously these attributive notations remain much closer to the practical than the symbolic. Still, even these simple didascalia emerge as important signifiers, guiding the nature of mimesis in its more basic performative patterns.

The Structural Didascalia

Structural didascalia demarcate the play into "units such as acts and scenes" and are, next to the didascalia of attribution just mentioned, the most common (Carlson, p. 39). Although in such brief plays as *I Can't Remember Anything* or his 1991 *The Last Yankee* he has no practical or symbolic need for structural didascalia, Miller seems comfortable in most of his full-length plays with exploring the metaphorical possibilities implicit in dividing his scripts into plainly demarcated "acts." He divides *The Crucible*, for instance, into four acts, ending each with the didascalic notation, "THE CURTAIN FALLS"; but when the curtain descends, casting its own shadows, the audience cannot help but realize that much more than a curtain falls for Abigail or Proctor. The descending curtain itself is much more than a mere curtain; visually, the curtain becomes another part of Miller's subtextual language, reinforcing our sense of the moral divisions that are such an important part of Miller's ideographic backdrop within *The Crucible*.

The Locational Didascalia

Complementing the structural stage directions, the *locational* didascalia "are often connected with textual announcements of new scenes or new acts" (Carlson, pp. 37-38). From such elementary locational notations as "*another part of the forest*" or, in *A View from the Bridge*, "*Rodolpho appears in the bedroom doorway*,"[6] the locational didascalia in most modern American dramas are almost a given. Copious descriptions of the physical set and setting typically precede dialogue. In most of her plays--*Trifles*, *The Outside*, *The Verge*, and *Inheritors*, for instance--Susan Glaspell carefully delineates her locational didascalia, a practice that her Provincetown counterpart, Eugene O'Neill, would greatly expand upon. Maria Irene Fornes's *The Danube* could hardly be understood without its locational (and other) forms of didascalia. Similarly, such playwrighting methodology intrigues Miller, for virtually all of his major plays open with careful locational notations, notations that sometimes capture what Miller calls "the primitiveness of the image-story" (*Everybody Wins*, p. xi). For example, he begins Act I of *Salesman* with two pages of textured locational didascalia:

> *A melody is heard, played upon a flute. It is small and fine, telling of grass and trees and the horizon. The curtain rises.*
>
> *Before us is the Salesman's house. We are aware of towering, angular shapes behind it, surrounding it on all sides. Only the blue light of the sky falls upon the house and forestage; the surrounding area shows an angry glow of orange. As more light appears, we see a solid vault of apartment houses around the small, fragile-seeming home.*[7]

So, too, with *After the Fall*, where "*The action takes place in the mind, thought, and memory of Quentin.*"[8] And so forth until Linda Loman and Quentin, respectively, deliver their opening lines. It would be unthinkable (or at least curious) to ignore Miller's opening descriptions, for they establish, not only the set and setting, but, more provocatively, the tone and theme, the physical and metaphysical patterns that infiltrate all visible action that follows. More than being mere minor descriptions of set and setting, then, the locational didascalia function in *Salesman* as an architectural monument to and psychological projection of the Lomans' spiritual predicament. Often Miller's heroes appear as frustrated with their settings as did Tom Wingfield in Williams's *The Glass Menagerie*, whose apartment stands as "*one of those vast hive-like conglomerations of cellular living units.*"[9] Hence Willy's once-brightly painted home has faded with his dream into the "Bricks and windows, windows and bricks" (*Salesman*, p. 17), which sparks one of his many tirades: "The street is lined with cars. There's not a breath of fresh air in the neighborhood. The grass don't grow any more, you can't raise a carrot in the back yard. They should've had a law against apartment houses" (*Salesman*, p. 17).

The Didascalia of Character Description

Complementing the locational didascalia, particularly in modern drama, are the didascalia of *character description*. Often appearing at the very start of the play, or sometimes at the point of a character's first stage appearance, character descriptions have become surprisingly helpful in providing scholars and actors with richly coded emblems relative to how we may construct "the proper mental picturization" of a key character (Carlson, p. 37). Such didascalia go well beyond mere external description; they also provide symbolic codes that reveal much about the inner consciousness of the character. In his screenplay *Everybody Wins*, Miller feels the medium of film invites minimalist character descriptions; he introduces Angela, played by Debra Winger, thus: "*high heels rapping, comes running up the street to him, already waving, wearing a low-cut dress and makeup too heavy for the morning, and carrying an incongruous attache case in one hand, a fresh newspaper in the other*" (p. 4). By contrast, in *The Crucible, Incident at Vichy*, and *The Price*, the specificity with which Miller describes the characters seems part of Miller's stratagem for bridging theoretical as well as practical gaps within the text/performance dialectic. Perhaps inspired not only by Ibsen but by his contemporaries O'Neill and Williams, Miller pays great attention to his character descriptions, descriptions that enable readers, directors, actors, critics, and audiences to comprehend more adequately, not merely what Willy Loman looks like, but what defines the nature of Willy's sensibilities, values, and his very being itself. Miller's character descriptions surely helped Elia Kazan and Jo Mielziner conceptualize each character's "spine," as Kazan called it, and the play's multivalent set and lighting. One of Miller's best character descriptions concerns his didascalic portrait of Linda Loman, a portrait transcending mere physicality:

> *Linda, his wife, has stirred in her bed at the right. She gets out and puts on a robe, listening. Most often jovial, she has developed an iron repression of her expectations to Willy's behavior--she more than loves him, she admires him, as though his mercurial nature, his temper, his massive dreams and little cruelties, served her only as sharp reminders of the turbulent longings within him, longings which she shares but lacks the temperament to utter and follow to their end. (Salesman,* p. 12)

At times Miller provides, during the closure of *After the Fall*, for example, a description that can only be internalized by the actress playing Maggie, who "*rises from the floor webbed with demons, trying to awake*" (p. 128). Miller sometimes gives even minor characters healthy descriptions, didascalia that mentally and aurally help us better understand, not merely the characters' psychology but the implicit values underpinning their motivations and actions.

The Performance Didascalia

Among the many other types of stage directions, *performance* didascalia are embedded throughout Miller's texts. As Carlson points out, "these have to do with the actual happenings on stage. A few are technical, noting lighting changes, sounds, the movement of objects, and so on, but most concern the conduct of actors on stage" (p. 39). Michael Issacharoff calls these "visual didascalia," for they have to do with kinesic and proxemic concerns, and with such issues as costuming and other non-verbal gestures, props, and codes.[10] Therefore even the title of each Miller play can be viewed as part of the didascalic discourse, as can such other details as the theater program the usher gives one in the lobby, the posters advertising the play, and certainly the theater space itself. Stylistic analysis of the majority of Miller's plays reveals just to what extent he relies on performance didascalia: to cite but two illustrations, of the 139 pages of text making of the Viking paperback edition of *Salesman* 139 contain performance (or in a few rare instances, other kinds of) didascalia; of the 129 pages in *After the Fall*, 129 contain some form of subtextual discourse. Miller's performance didascalia may be as simple as when Kroll in *Clara* "(*Looks confused*)";[11] when Angela in *Some Kind of Love Story* speaks "(*Incredulously*)";[12] when Maggie in *After the Fall* is *suddenly brightening*" (p. 89); or as suggestive as in the following moment that climaxes Act II in *Salesman*:

> *As the car speeds off, the music crashes down in a frenzy of sound, which becomes the soft pulsation of a single cello string. Biff slowly returns to his bedroom. He and Happy gravely don their jackets. Linda slowly walks out of her room. The music has developed into a dead march. The leaves of the day are appearing over everything. Charley and Bernard, somberly dressed, appear. . . . All stare down at the grave. (p. 136)*

It seems as if the dramatist Miller feels compelled to provide what in fictive discourse is the omniscient narrator. If Miller's didascalia are ultimately unable to control (or at least guide) a contemporary director's version of *Salesman* (which, to be sure, could lead to an exciting new staging of an old classic), at least they may indicate to both director and actor the spirit of Miller's original dramaturgic intents.

Theatrical Implications

So what are we to make of didascalic discourse and its relationship to textuality and theatricality in his theater? The conspicuous presence of stage directions animates--almost as much as the dialogue--his plays. Between one-quarter and one-third of each Miller playtext appears as some type of stage direction. As we celebrate the many faces of Arthur Miller, then, what might be the final implications of his lengthy didascalia? Increasingly more theater troupes and readers may not be as familiar with the original version of *Salesman*, say, as was Elia Kazan. Or we can only imagine how crucial they were to the Chinese actors in the Beijing version. Further, as we near the next millennium, more and more directors feel compelled to alter, reinvent, modify the author's original conception of the performance. Indeed, sometimes this may enhance a play. And since theater emerges as such a collaborative effort, one may concede that a playwright may allow directors some creative leeway to subvert the authority of the script. Surely no one would doubt that Kazan's directorial prowess only enhanced the 1949 version of *Death of a Salesman*.

But problems--theatrical and even legal--may be present. For example, JoAnne Akalaitis, director of a 1984 version of Beckett's *Endgame* for the American Repertory Theatre, altered the set. Beckett was so disturbed he threatened legal action. The Beckett controversy resurfaced in 1988, at the *Comedie Francaise*, when director Giles Bourdet changed slightly the color of the set of *Endgame*. What seems fascinating is that in both instances, not a single word-change was in question. Rather, Beckett challenged the directors' proposed modifications in his didascalia--the play's described setting.[13]

The best example in Miller's case is, of course, the Wooster Group's controversial versions of *The Crucible*. Inspired by Elizabeth LeCompte, the Wooster Group wrote to Dramatists Play Service for performance rights in 1982, only to be denied. As David Savran and Ruby Cohn have pointed out, in 1982-84 LeCompte wrote Miller's agent, dealt with lawyers, and in February 1983 rehearsals of *L.S.D.* began, a play that included some 45 minutes of lines from *The Crucible*.[14] Miller himself watched some rehearsals--where the men in the play were dressed in contemporary clothes, complete with microphones, in Miller's altered (or deconstructed if you prefer) text. Although Miller at first seemed willing to grant permission, he refused in late 1983. LeCompte wrote three letters to Miller while the Wooster Group continued to develop *L.S.D.* The controversy continued in 1985 with the Wooster Group receiving from Miller's attorney a "cease-and-desist" order, which closed the show. Finally, in 1986 the issue was somehow resolved, with the production entitled, *The Road to Immortality (Part 2)*. Although, as Savran and Cohn observe, *The Crucible* was distilled to one line, the aesthetic questions both Miller and the Wooster Group raised (not to mention questions of censorship) were wedded to a faithful reading of Miller's subtext. Miller feared the Group, in its goal of repackaging Miller's lines "in their own words," would distort his play too much.

Perhaps this explains why Miller, like Beckett in *Act Without Words I* and *II*, overdetermines his playscripts with an incredible amount of stage notations. While there remains much room for directorial interpretation and transformational acting in his theater, Miller seems unwilling to abdicate much authorial control. If Pirandello in *Six Characters in Search of an Author* invites spontaneity and alterations in live performance (despite the textual fact that of the 2,412 lines making up the *Naked Masks* version of the play, 805 are didascalia), Miller seems drawn toward seeing his plays the way he originally conceived of them. And the didascalia, rendered invisible when performed, enable Miller to establish, if not always maintain, such theatrical control.

Miller's subtextual discourse transcends a secondary textual status, standing much closer to the center of mimesis than many recognize. In text, his didascalia will forever remain in brackets, but once those stage directions interfold themselves in live spectacle, they become an indispensable part of a total performance. Further if directors and actors of a Miller play honor the spirit as well as the specifics of the didascalia, emblematic patterns will not be diminished, but enhanced. "Things go differently on a stage," Miller reminds us. He adds:

> Set a phone on a table under a light and raise the curtain, and in complete silence, after a few minutes, something will accrete around it. Questions and anticipations will begin to emanate from it, we will begin to imagine meanings in its isolation--in a word, the phone becomes an incipient metaphor. (*Everybody Wins*, p. vi)

Such accretions define the subtextual dimensions of Miller's theater. If performers and readers alike wish to re-stage any Miller play as close to the original, interfolding the multilayered functions of didascalia may be the first step toward replicating both the simple physical gesture as well as the complex moral seriousness that appear crucial to any Miller play. After all, Miller tells us, "a description in words tends to inflate, expand, and inflame the imagination, so that in the end the thing or person described is amplified into a larger-than-life figment" (*Everybody Wins*, p. v). The descriptions upon which Miller reflects emanate as much from Miller's subtext as they do from the audible dialogue itself.

Perhaps it seems fitting to close by returning to the Ancients and their use of the term didascalia. This term originated from the Greek word *didaskein*, which means "to teach." Another important derivative, *didascalian*, translates to "what should be taught" or "things that should be taught." Since Miller does not use a Hellenic chorus nor a Tieresias to comment upon a character's moral choice or his hubris, the "teaching" force in his theater first appears in the scripted page version. In the spirit of "teaching" actors how to perform a Miller scene, the didascalia become central, rather than other, to performance. To be sure, most directors, actors, and critics certainly read over Miller's didascalia, but most professional actors and directors ultimately ignore, or at least marginalize, the performative status of the didascalia. After all, they seem to be merely convenient reminders of how to gesture or when to exit, reminders that, through rehearsals, become interiorized, their invisibility part of the magic of re-presenting Miller's mimetics. Once internalized, the didascalia are viewed by their absences, replaced as they are by the body language of the actors and his or her presentation of a character's crisis. Still, it seems the didascalia exert a profound influence on both text and performance: they bear directly on questions of representation and dramatic textualization.

Remaining tantalizingly ambiguous in their page and stage versions, the didascalia seem destined to linger near the borders of written and spoken discourse, but will undeniably remain at the center of interpretive control and audience reception of any Miller play. As we turn our spectators' gaze to the many faces of Arthur Miller, however, perhaps such subtextual ambiguity delights us most when viewing his theater.

Notes

[1] Arthur Miller, *Everybody Wins* (New York: Grove Weidenfeld, 1990), p. vi. All further references will appear in the text.

[2] Michael Issacharoff and Robin F. Jones, *Performing Texts* (Philadelphia: University of Pennsylvania Press, 1988), p. 1.

[3] Marvin Carlson, "The Status of Stage Directions," *Studies in the Literary Imagination*, 24 (Fall 1991), 37-48. For a more detailed account of the status and function of the didascalia, see Roman Ingarden, *The Literary Work of Art: An Investigation on the Borderlines on Ontology, Logic, and Theory of Literature*, trans. by George G. Grabowicz (Evanston: Northwestern University Press, 1973), pp. 208-10; Keir Elan, *Semiotics of Theatre and Drama* (London: Methuen, 1980), pp. 33-37; Michael Issacharoff, *Discourse as Performance* (Stanford: Stanford University Press, 1989), pp. 16-27; and Manfred Pfister, *The Theory and Analysis of Drama*, trans. by John Halliday (Cambridge: Cambridge University Press, 1988), pp. 13-22, 30-38, 40-48. For the purpose of this essay, however, I am most indebted to Marvin Carlson. I rely on Carlson's typological model of the major forms of didascalia, and I gratefully acknowledge his excellent work here. All further references to Carlson's work will appear in the text.

[4] Arthur Miller, *Incident at Vichy* (New York: Penguin, 1965), p. 18.

[5] Arthur Miller, *The Price*, in *Arthur Miller's Collected Plays* (New York: Viking, 1981), II, p. 313.

[6] Arthur Miller, *A View from the Bridge* (New York: Penguin, 1961), p. 63.

[7] Arthur Miller, *Death of a Salesman* (New York: Viking, 1950), p. 11. All further references to this work will appear in the text.

[8] Arthur Miller, *After the Fall* (New York: Viking, 1964), p. 1. All further references to this work will appear in the text.

[9] Tennessee Williams, *The Glass Menagerie* (New York: Signet, 1987), p. 27.

[10] Michael Issacharoff, "Stage Codes" in *Performing Texts*, pp. 61-65.

[11] Arthur Miller, *Clara* in *Danger: Memory!* (New York: Grove, 1987), p. 44.

[12] Arthur Miller, *Some Kind of Love Story* (New York: Dramatists Play Service, 1983), p. 21.

[13] See Patricia A Suchy, "When Worlds Collide: The Stage Direction as Utterance," *Journal of Dramatic Theory and Criticism*, 6 (Fall 1992), 69-82 and Carlson's essay, pp. 44-46, for concise and extremely helpful discussions of the

Beckett controversy. Further, Suchy's essay extends Carlson's discussion of the performative status of the didascalia.

[14] See Ruby Cohn, "Which Is Witch?" in *Public Issues, Private Tensions: Contemporary American Drama*, ed. Matthew C. Roudané (New York: AMS Press, 1993). Cohn provides a succinct chronology of the Wooster Group-Miller controversy, which I draw upon here. See also David Savran, *Breaking the Rules: The Wooster Group* (New York: TCG, 1988) and Alexis Greene, "Elizabeth LeCompte and the Wooster Group" in *Contemporary American Theatre*, ed. Bruce King (New York: St. Martin's, 1991), pp. 117-34.

Fathers and Sons in
They Too Arise

James A. Robinson

In a 1966 interview, Arthur Miller described the father-son relationship as "a very primitive thing in my plays" because "the father was really a figure who incorporated both power and some kind of moral law which he had either broken or had fallen prey to."[1] Miller's association of the father with moral law is revealing, for it suggests a specific indebtedness to a Jewish heritage which his theatrical work in general has obscured. However resolutely non-ethnic Miller's plays may be, Judaism helps account for the anthrocentricity of Miller's vision, and his preoccupation with the moral issues dramatized by the numerous father-son conflicts in his plays. In *All My Sons*, Joe Keller has violated a moral law, symbolically killing one son and ultimately outraging the other; Willy Loman falls prey to a specifically American "moral law," that self-worth depends upon material success, and provokes the rebellion of his son Biff. For both fathers, that filial rebellion is heartbreaking; for as the Jewish son of a Jewish immigrant, Miller secretly yearns for the reassuring historical continuity that the transmission of a paternal legacy signifies. But as an American, he simultaneously projects in his drama a revolt against paternal authority; and as a liberal heir of Karl Marx, he dreams of brotherhood triumphing over fatherhood. All of these contending elements appear in Miller's first play, written while he was a Michigan undergraduate: *They Too Arise*. And an examination of this play will shed some light on the struggles between fatherhood and brotherhood in later plays, and on the issue of Miller's desired--but incomplete--assimilation into mainstream American culture.

They Too Arise is Miller's most nakedly autobiographical play, both in language and characters.[2] The Simon family of New York speak in an urban Jewish dialect; the family structure duplicates Miller's birth family, consisting of a father, mother, two brothers, and a younger sister; the protagonist, Abe Simon, physically resembles Isidore Miller ("ruddy and fair, with a solid strength in his face"); and he is also a formerly prosperous coat manufacturer, now (in 1935) facing financial difficulty due to the Depression. He cannot afford to pay for the trip home of his son Arnold, an undergraduate (like Arthur Miller at the time) at the University of Michigan. Abe's older son, Ben, has had to abandon college to work in his father's small factory, and Abe's family has been forced to move in with his wife's father. The latter situation causes conflict between patriarch and son-in-law over who makes final decisions in the house. As Abe laments in the opening scene, "when a man pays all the bills in a house he deserves to be the boss." Thus, at the outset of his playwrighting career Miller connects paternal power to economic issues: Abe's reduced earning power constitutes a loss of authority in his own eyes.

But he still asserts control over his sons. Abe asks that Ben accept an arranged marriage to Helen Roth, the daughter of a wealthy competitor, and that Arnold work over the summer at the factory--despite Arnold's leftist sympathy toward an impeding strike against all New York coat manufacturers, including his father. Arnold's resistance confuses and angers his parents. "In my day, when a father needed help all he had to do was open his mouth, and like that! He got it, no questions asked," Abe insists. "When you got sons, they help you." Thus, Miller articulates through Abe the ethic of filial obedience espoused by Judaism. Abe's wife, Esther, alludes to another Jewish value when she interprets the business to Arnold as an institution that affirms family--particularly male--continuity: "Your father, his father, the whole family since they came to America, even my family is [sic] been in the cloak business." And, though personally reluctant to force Ben's marriage, Abe appeals to him (in words echoed eleven years later in *All My Sons*) as male heir: "I wanna leave you with a . . . with a name . . . with a clean name and a . . . and a healthy business." Significantly, each brother tries to prevent his sibling's acceding to the father's request: acting out of love, they are brothers in more than name, representing the principle of brotherhood itself. But both give in, as Arnold ends up working in his father's factory, and Ben agrees to marry Helen Roth.

When the scene shifts to a meeting of the coat manufacturers' association, it becomes apparent that Abe is also a victim. He is one of the "little guys" earning less than $5000 a year, and he resists the desire of the large manufacturers to hire gangsters as strikebreakers because, he claims, "it ain't the way for Jewish men to act"--despite the possibility of financial ruin for Abe if the strike succeeds. His motives are personal as well as moral: Arnold has revolted against his father, and is now on the picket line, where he may be physically beaten by the strikebreakers. A second revolt against patriarchal authority is enacted in the following scene by Abe himself. He returns home to argue with his father-in-law, Poppa, a devout Jew who believes that

Arnold should never have been allowed to go to Michigan because his secular education has encouraged his current disobedience of his father. When Grandfather launches into a tirade about Abe's failure to take his advice or make enough money, Abe pushes him. At the close of the next scene, Abe learns of Grandfather's death. As both father and son, then, Abe is involved in a developing pattern of disrespect toward father figures within the play.

Abe's business situation grows more desperate in the final act, when the bank threatens to foreclose after his customers defect to the major manufacturers--whose use of gangster strikebreakers guarantees delivery of the customers' orders. After he learns that Roth (who is using strikebreakers) has unwittingly taken some of his orders, Abe cancels Ben's engagement to Roth's daughter, and experiences a birth of social awareness that aligns him with his sons. "Something rotten was pushing me," he tells his wife in reference to his attack on Poppa,

> and I know it even better now when I see what a man like Roth's gotta do to stay where he is! I know it, Esther, and it's gotta be wiped out! . . . I will not see my sons laughing at it the way I did till it drags them so far they gotta hit an old man to stand up! . . . we got six good arms and three good heads. We oughta be able to learn a lot . . . we can change a lot with such . . . with such equipment. A lotta changing we can do . . . a lotta changing.

Though the antecedent of "it" appears to shift in the third sentence, Miller (like Odets in *Awake and Sing!*, produced the same year) seems to be decrying an obsession with money that results in betrayal of one's family members--whether father-in-law or son.

They Too Arise offers several interesting variations on the themes of paternal authority and filial disobedience. At the beginning, Abe represents a patriarchal power (stretching back to the preceding male generation) that is connected to the "cloak business," that is, to economic power. To Abe, economic and moral authority appear identical: "when a man pays all the bills in the house he deserves to be boss." In other words, Abe (from Miller's liberal perspective) is an unquestioning capitalist. Abe's assumption is clearly challenged, however, when the large manufacturers (economically more powerful than he) ask him to hire gangsters, an act that would both violate his morality and threaten his younger son. The coincidence of the two consequences is important, for the play--like the later *All My Sons*--connects morality *to* the sons, who represent a principle of brotherhood. Both of them initially sacrifice for the father, bowing to his authority; but both feel uncomfortable in the business world, and try to defend one another from the demands made by Abe. Ultimately, the younger son breaks from the paternal authority in his decision to join the picket line: another assertion of brotherhood, this time in the public sphere. This sets in motion the chain of events that ultimately cause the father to recant his equation of economic and moral power. Abe comes to realize "this way we got of eating each other ... it's no way, Esther! They [Ben and Arnold] got a life to live! ... I'm gonna see to it they don't waste it like I did trying to get rich!" (my ellipses) In effect, Abe here redefines his concept of paternal legacy. No longer is it necessary to pass on a "healthy business," as he had attempted via Ben's arranged marriage to Helen Roth; it now becomes more vital to be a model of moral integrity for one's sons, and to thereby pass on a code of ethical behavior.

That code, however, emanates from two contradictory male sources. The first is that of the sons themselves, especially Arnold, who places concern for social justice above the economic expediency at first championed by Abe. Arn's assault on paternal authority helps reconstitute it, succeeds in making a "brother" out of his father, for Abe finally joins Ben and Arn in their liberal revolt. The second source is Poppa, a man of "majestic carriage" who engages in daily worship of God. Symbolically, Poppa's religious practice helps account for Abe's explanation of his resistance to the hiring of gangsters: "it ain't the way for Jewish men to act." Abe explicitly aligns himself with the Judaic tradition of righteousness and decency Poppa represents. But Poppa is also the man who--in his narrow defense of his religion-- berates Abe for permitting the secular education of Ben and (especially) Arn, which he believes has prompted their filial rebellion. In other words, in his anti-assimilationism, he opposes the process which instigated Arn's filial revolt--the revolt which helped spur Abe's ultimate alliance with his sons, in an implicit affirmation of the moral decency Poppa himself represents. And, equally paradoxically, it is Abe's shame over his brief physical assault on Poppa ("something rotten was pushing me")--an act of filial disobedience--that provides the catalyst for the conversion experience that aligns him with Poppa's morality.

They Too Arise exhibits considerable ambivalence, then, toward the authority of Jewish fathers and forefathers. Obviously, Miller respects the moral essence of the Judaic code Poppa stands for, because it enables Abe to resist in engaging in shady activities and to reclaim his integrity at the end. Like Joe Keller and Willy Loman, Abe has been pushed toward corruption by a capitalistic system that encourages moral compromise in the pursuit of economic survival; unlike them, he is saved by his identification with an ethnic tradition where ethics are central. But that same Old World tradition (as represented by Poppa, at any rate) views American secular education as a threat to the respect a Jewish son owes his father--and hence, an implicit threat to the continuity between male generations that has ensured the survival of the Jewish faith for thousands of years. He is right to be concerned. Arnold's disobedience of his father, a product of his exposure to liberal and socialist ideas at college, does indeed threaten their relationship (and helps bring down Abe's business as well). We might recall Miller's words in *Time-bends*: "deep down in the comradely world of the Marxist promise is parri-cide."[3] Moreover, neither Arnold nor Ben practices his religion or identifies with his ethnic background. The situation was (and is) common among American Jews. As Marshall Sklare has observed, educational mobility has indeed caused estrangement between Jewish parents and children, especially when the children become involved as a consequence in "radical politics," whereby "the child comes to participate in a world that is different from that of his parents. . . . Inevitably, the ties which bind the individual to his kin are loosened."[4] But Miller (a college student when he wrote the play) clearly does not consider this an important problem. Though Abe desires his sons' obedience, even he does not regard this as a religious issue, as a conse-quence of his own assimilation into secular American culture via his business. And Miller attempts to dissolve the remaining grounds of conflict between generations (over business practices) by engineering Abe's reconciliation with his sons--on their terms--at the end.

Abe's conversion (like Ralph's in *Awake and Sing*) taxes one's credulity somewhat. A man who has prospered in business does not so easily see the company go under, or become more liberal as a consequence of a moral epi-phany. But Abe's transformation serves the purpose of promoting Miller's quintessentially American (and liberal) belief in the healthiness of the sons' rebellion against the father. In marked contrast to the later tragedies, the filial rebellion is rendered unproblematic. In *Sons* and *Salesman*, the father perishes, as a direct consequence of a son's assault on him for the corruption of his values by American capitalism; here the father repents, recants, and survives to join his sons. The play's conclusion--the product not just of Miller's youth, but of the implicit demand for upbeat endings in leftist plays at the time--demonstrates Miller's optimism that initially opposing demands of fatherhood and brotherhood can be reconciled.

But it achieves their reconciliation by two intriguing devices. The first is the death of Poppa, which effectively rids the play of its most principled proponent of filial obedience. His demise symbolically frees the father Abe from insistence on his paternal authority: hence, it is appropriate that the son-in-law's own assault help bring about the patriarch's death. More broadly, that death also suggests Miller's desire at the time to assimilate fully into American culture. Though Arnold is presented as having a close rela-tionship with Poppa, adherence to Poppa's old-fashioned, anti-assimilationist mentality would effectively prevent not only Arnold's political liberation, but also his ability to transcend his ethnic roots. To prevent Arnold from experiencing any guilt about this desired transcendence, Miller makes Abe the agent of Poppa's death. Ironically, Abe's guilt feelings over the role he plays help return him (as mentioned) to the positive aspects of the Jewish morality Poppa represents--thereby helping to restore the continuity between father and son that Arnold's and Abe's rebellions threatened to disrupt. *They Too Arise* thus effectively retains and combines two essential aspects of Judaism--its morality and emphasis on male continuity; but it transforms both by secularizing them, divesting them of any religious justifications or associations. Abe's legacy is one of integrity, not of religious belief.

The second unusual aspect of the father/son reconciliation is that it is effected by the father's ultimate surrender of his position to his sons. The two boys, representing brotherhood not only in their personal relationship but also in their behavior, are presented as wiser, more just, than their father. In effect, they become Abe's father, inverting the usual relationship; and Abe joins them as essentially a brother in the fight against the corruptions of capitalism at the end. A variation on the same pattern obtains in *Sons* and *Salesman*, where Chris Keller and Biff Loman become teachers of their fathers, opening their eyes to moral connections between events which they have been unable to see or admit. But in the later, tragic dramas, the truth costs Joe Keller and Willy Loman their lives. Here, a much younger Miller, full of hope (like many young men during the Depression), minimizes the price that must be paid. If the later plays strike one as too hard, even melodramatic, in their punishing resolutions, *They Too Arise* seems too easy. The conflict between the principle of fatherhood--with its insistence on hierarchy and subordination--and the principle of brotherhood--with its valorization of love and mutual sacrifice--is not so simply reconciled. Ultimately, father here simply (and unrealistically) concedes the battle to the son; and it is not altogether surprising, given the unconvincing reversal and highly rhetorical speeches of the last scene, that the play remains both unproduced and unpublished.

Despite its flaws, *They Too Arise* constitutes an interesting opening treatment of the father/son relationship in Miller's body of work. As a first play, it perhaps inevitably draws on Miller's personal background more than any subsequent drama except *The American Clock*. In doing so, it reveals the centrality of male relationships (both filial and fraternal), and how the world of work affects those male bonds: two concerns that appear repeatedly in his later plays. Unique in its depiction of Miller's Jewish ethnic background, the play nonetheless exhibits his desire to transcend that background while retaining its moral teachings: again, a description that applies equally to his subsequent plays. Its plot also implies the value placed by Miller, as a Jew, on male generational continuity, despite the power of social and economic forces--Arnold's education, the Depression--that threaten that continuity by turning son against father. Finally, it dramatizes the attraction of Miller to brotherhood, and how devotion to one's brothers (whether actual or metaphorical) can threaten obedience to the father and the traditional authority for which he stands. In other words, *They Too Arise* functions in several respects as a model for the more accomplished dramas that follow: it puts a political spin on essentially autobiographical (and fundamentally Jewish) material, pointing finally to the archetypal conflict between father and son that gives his work much of its depth and its power.

Notes

[1] Arthur Miller, in Interview with Olga Carlisle and Rose Styron, "The Art of the Theatre II: Arthur Miller, An Interview," in *Conversations with Arthur Miller*, ed. Matthew C. Roudané (Jackson: University of Mississippi Press, 1987), pp. 89-90.

[2] There are several versions of *They Too Arise* under various titles, including *No Villain* (its original title, under which it won an Avery Hopwood Award at Michigan) and *The Grass Still Grows* (when Miller revised it as a comedy). My argument takes as its text the typescript of *They Too Arise* in the Miller collection at the Harry Crowe Ransom Humanities Research Center at the University of Texas at Austin. All quotations are from that typescript.

[3] Arthur Miller, *Timebends* (New York: Grove, 1987), p. 111.

[4] Marshall Sklare, *America's Jews* (New York: Random House, 1971), pp. 90-91. For further discussion of Miller as a Jewish playwright, see Morris Freedman, "The Jewishness of Arthur Miller," in *American Drama in Social Context* (Carbondale: Southern Illinois University Press, 1971), pp. 43-58; Enoch Brater, "Ethics and Ethnicity in the Plays of Arthur Miller," in Sarah B. Cohen, ed., *From Hester Street to Hollywood: The Jewish-American Stage and Screen* (Bloomington: Indiana University Press, 1983), pp. 123-34; and my "*All My Sons* and Paternal Authority," *Journal of American Drama and Theatre*, 2, No. 1 (Winter 1990), 38-54.

The Reformation of Biff Loman:
A View from the Pre-Production Scripts

Brenda Murphy

In the introduction to his *Collected Plays*, Arthur Miller wrote that he had attempted in *Death of a Salesman* to counteract what he called the "law of success," to which Willy Loman succumbs, with "an opposing system which, so to speak, is in a race for Willy's faith . . . the system of love which is the opposite of the law of success."[1] Miller suggests that the system of love "is embodied in Biff Loman, but by the time Willy can perceive his love it can serve only as an ironic comment upon the life he sacrificed for power and for success and its tokens" (Introduction, p. 36).

But Miller has expressed his own disappointment, shared by most critics of the play, that Biff's "self-realization . . . is not a weightier counterbalance to Willy's disaster in the audience's mind,"[2] a problem that may arise from the weakness of the play's representation of Biff's value-system in contrast with the powerfully presented success myth. Whereas the law of success is omnipresent in the play, constantly reminding the spectator of its pervasiveness in the culture that has produced Willy and his sons, Biff's mature love for Willy is presented for consideration only in the climactic scene, when Biff embraces Willy and pleads with him to "take that phony dream and burn it before something happens."[3] As Biff starts away, Willy says, "Isn't that--isn't that remarkable? Biff--he likes me!" (*Salesman*, p. 133), and Linda responds, "He loves you, Willy!" (*Salesman*, p. 133).

The climactic power of this moment as a point of Aristotelian recognition is severely undercut, however. Willy does not make the leap of understanding about the falsity of the success myth that Biff is trying to force. Instead, Miller uses irony to suggest his continued blindness, as, "*choking with his love*," Willy "*cries out his promise*: That boy--that boy is going to be magnificent" (*Salesman*, p. 133). It is Willy's continued belief in the law of success, and in Biff's ability to fulfill it, that provides the immediate motive for his suicide--the $20,000 that will finance Biff's rise in business. Beneath this obvious irony is the inadequacy of the love that Biff is offering his desperate father. To prove his love, Biff plans to go away in the morning, never to return. Willy's faith in the law of success may have destroyed him, but Biff's form of love would leave his father to a bleak, perhaps poverty-stricken future, with only the feckless Hap to depend on. As a counter to the inhumanity of the callous business system that "eat[s] the orange and throw[s] the peel away" (*Salesman*, p. 82), Biff's value-system is far from adequate.

One reason for this inadequacy is that Biff was not originally intended to be a moral counterforce to Willy. In all of the play's pre-production versions, Biff's character was far less virtuous and a good deal more like Willy's than it is in the published version. In fact, it was well into the rehearsal process that Miller actually wrote the climactic scene as it now appears, putting Biff's revelation of love at its center.

In the Miller Collection at the University of Texas, there is a carbon copy of a *Salesman* script with revisions printed in pencil. Written on the title page is "Miller's Script" and "This is my final script but one;--includes some obvious work that did not survive rehearsal, and scenes which were later added and reshaped   Arthur Miller."[4] This version was followed by another typed version before the script was "frozen" for the actors, but was used in the earliest stages of rehearsal, while Miller worked closely with director Elia Kazan and the actors to give the play its final shape. In this early script, Biff is notably more like his father and brother than he is in the published version, particularly in two ways, his sexuality and his compulsive lying to put the best face on his actions. He is also a compulsive thief and a convicted felon, characteristics that were smoothed over or expunged in the remaking of Biff for the final script.

In the earlier version, the young Hap and Biff tell Willy about a hike that Biff has led the other boys on. When Willy asks them what kind of "adventures" they had, Biff replies, "Well, we pitched camp in an apple orchard and . . . a girl came around, Dad" (R, p. 1-37). Willy laughs, and Hap says, "Biff was with her in the tent," to which Willy replies "(Proudly, attempting a wry reprimand) No! Biff!" and Biff says, "(Smiling proudly) She just wouldn't let me go, Dad." The scene continues:

> Willy: That so! (Teeming with sensuous happiness) Picked you out of all the boys, heh?
> Biff: Yeah, Dad.
> Willy: How old was she?
> Biff: Oh, about . . . forty.
> Willy: That so! How about Bernard, did he . . . ?
> Biff: Oh, Bernard! He was blushing all the time, and anyway she wouldn't even look at him.

Willy: (With a joyous attempt at pity) Bernard is not well-liked, is he. (R, pp. 1-37-38)

The scene established several characteristics of the Lomans that are familiar from the published script: Willy's pride in Biff's popularity, his competition with Charley and Bernard, and the sensuality of the Loman men, coupled with their depersonalization of women. It suggests more overtly than any scene in the published play that Hap and Biff have absorbed their attitudes about sex and women directly from Willy. It also presents Biff as a much less innocent boy than he appears in the final script. It would strain the audience's credulity to suggest that the boy who casually "scored" with women in tents would be emotionally shattered when confronted with the occasional dalliance of his travelling-salesman father, particularly when he was used to boasting to him of his conquests. In that sense, the Biff of the final script is more consistent as a character, but the Biff in the cut scene is perhaps more believable as a Loman.

As he revised the script, Miller made a number of changes that set up a contrast between Hap's attitude toward women and Biff's. For example, in the earlier script, when Hap asks Biff if he's interested in Miss Forsythe, Biff replies, "I never speared anything like that" (R). And later in the scene, when he gets angry with Willy and wants to leave, he says, "Where's that woman? I'm going diving tonight" (R). In the published script, Hap takes all the initiative with the women, and Biff seems to have been living an almost monastic life out west.

The most important change in Biff's character, however, was centered on the incident with Bill Oliver and Biff's narration of it. In the published script, Biff tells Hap in the restaurant before Willy arrives that Oliver had seen him for one minute and walked away after Biff had waited in his office for six hours. "He comes out. Didn't remember who I was or anything," Biff says. "I felt like such an idiot" (*Salesman*, p. 104). Then Biff explains that he went into Oliver's office, took his fountain pen, and ran down all eleven flights to the street. When Biff tells Hap that he intends to tell Willy the truth about this, Hap persuades him to make up the story about having a lunch date with Oliver so that Willy will have something to hope for. When Willy arrives, Biff starts to tell him the truth, but is pressured by Willy's having been fired into using Hap's story. Biff tells Willy about stealing the pen, however, and says he can't keep the appointment with Oliver. When Willy and Hap quite naturally try to persuade Biff that he can toss off his having picked up the pen as an oversight, Biff says, "Listen, kid, I took those balls years ago, now I walk in with his fountain pen? That clinches it, don't you see? I can't face him like that!" (*Salesman*, p. 112). When Willy continues to pressure Biff, he tells him he has no appointment.

One problem with the restaurant scene as published is Biff's motivation. If he agrees to go along with Hap's lie in order to ease Willy's anxiety about having been fired, why would he upset Willy needlessly by saying that he can't keep the appointment because he stole the pen? And since he has already told Hap that Oliver didn't even remember him, the only motive for reminding Willy about the stolen basketballs would be to upset him further at a time when he was supposed to be setting his mind at ease. The inconsistency in Biff's motivation is partly due to Miller's extensive revision of the scene during rehearsals.[5] In the two versions of the script preceding the final rehearsal script, Biff does not reveal that he was lying about seeing Oliver until his final climactic confrontation with Willy. In the restaurant scene, Biff does not tell Happy the truth, but tells the lie about having an appointment with Oliver to both Hap and Willy. He says that Oliver remembered and welcomed him, that they discussed "the Florida deal," and that it was only "a question of the amount." Thus there is not the moral distinction between Biff and Hap that is made in the published version, and Biff's intention in the restaurant scene is to deceive Willy rather than to make him see the truth.

In the earlier versions, Biff's stealing is much more central to the scene, to his character, and to his relationship with Willy. In the story he tells about his meeting with Oliver, he says that he felt Oliver kept waiting for him to say something about his having stolen the basketballs. When Oliver went to consult with his partner, Biff says:

> I waited two minutes, five minutes . . . and it's gettin' to be about ten minutes, see? And it's after five. So I started getting sore, y'know. Because nobody is going to treat me that way, I don't care who he is. And I could just see him out there with his partner laughing at the big dope coming back to the place where he stole a box of basketballs and having the nerve to ask for ten thousand dollars. I even thought I *heard* laughter in the next office. (R, p. 2-46)

Biff says that he was doing a crossword puzzle while he was waiting and he took the pen because he was angry at Oliver and, more importantly, because he remembered that Willy's pen was broken. The scene continues:

> Biff: Here, take the pen.
> Willy: Why?
> Biff: It's for you, take it.
> Willy (Taking it.): It's a beautiful thing. (Biff bursts out laughing, stops short.) What are you laughing at?
> Biff: You don't care where I get anything, do you?
> Willy: You're not a thief.
> Biff: (With a broad vicious smile) I found it, heh? You're already convinced that I found it on Forty-second street. (R, p. 2-49)

Then Biff tells Willy that he had been in jail in Kansas City for stealing a suit and a hat, and "The suit I stole turned out to be your size. Isn't that a funny thing? The judge couldn't understand it and neither could I . . . but I'll be damned if the suit and the hat weren't your size" (R, p. 2-53).

This scene linked Biff's stealing much more overtly to Willy than the published version does, giving a rather pat psychological explanation for it. Still trying to please Willy, Biff lies and steals like the other Lomans, and not only is he on the same moral level as Hap, but he's also not as bright. As he says of Hap, "he's the same way in his heart, except he's too smart to do it that way. We're all thieves" (R, p. 2-53). In the context of this characterization of Biff, the story of the pen and its revelation make more sense. The restaurant scene has a clearer motivation. But there is no suggestion of an alternative value system to present to Willy's in their final confrontation.

In the published script, Biff approaches the final, climactic confrontation with Willy in the role of truth-teller. Twice as Willy tries to resuscitate the saving fantasy of Oliver, Biff gently reminds him, "I've got no appointment, Dad" (*Salesman*, pp. 128, 129). When Willy accuses him of cutting down his life for spite, Biff decides the time for basic truths has come. Laying the rubber tubing on the table in front of Willy, he says, "All right, phony! Then let's lay it on the line . . . you're going to hear the truth--what you are and what I am!" (*Salesman*, p. 130). Biff reveals that he has been in jail for stealing and has stolen himself out of every good job since high school (*Salesman*, p. 131). But this self-revelation is a lead into his deeper understanding that the Lomans "never told the truth for ten minutes in this house" (*Salesman*, p. 131) and his attempt to get Willy and Hap to accept the fact that they are all "a dime a dozen" (*Salesman*, p. 132). That the others don't share his recognition is part of the play's tragedy, but Biff's self-acceptance and his rejection of Willy's phony dream suggest hope for the future.

In the earlier version, Biff's revelation is not that he has stolen--a fact that has already been established as central to his character--but that his appointment with Oliver is a fabrication:

> Biff: (Viciously) Listen, phony!
> Linda: (She starts at him.) Your filthy mouth! [Slight pause. They are aghast at his breath and his fury.]
> Biff: I've got no appointment tomorrow!
> Willy: No appointment.
> Biff (With intense self-hate) No appointment. I've got nowhere to go tomorrow.
>   (R, p. 2-79)

When Willy refuses to believe him, Biff says,

> Once and for all, Willy . . . I got no appointment with Jonas. You know why? Because if I told anybody but you that I was going to ask a man for $10,000 they'd say I was crazy or a goddamned liar.
> Willy: The man idolized you!
> Biff: I'm telling *you* now! Only you would listen to that nonsense . . . you and him (Happy). Nobody else. Because only we don't know who we are. I'm a dime a dozen, Willy, and so are you . . . (R, p. 2-79)

In some ways, the earlier scene is more dramatic. Coming presumably as a surprise to the audience as well as to Willy, the revelation that the Oliver story is a lie reveals the power of the Loman collective fantasy over Biff. The earlier version dramatized his freeing himself from its grip rather than presenting him as a self-appointed savior for the others. As a meeting of father and son, its emotional climax is more authentic:

> Willy: You're a vengeful, spiteful snot. Now you can get the hell out of here, and if I catch you back in this house again I'll kill ya! (Biff is rocked by his adamancy, his hate. He stands there for a moment, then walks across the room and at the edge of it . . . Willy utters a sob, but stops himself. Biff turns to him, and then moves toward him . . . Willy is raising his arms as though to defend himself.) Go way, go way!
> Hap: (Starting to get between them) Goddamit, Biff!
> Biff: (He lunges for Willy, who cries out in fear--and catching him, hugs him tightly, and begins to weep with his head clamped into Willy's neck.)
> Willy: (Astonished, infected by Biff's emotion) What're doin'? What're you doin'? (He holds Biff's face, looking at Biff.) Why is he crying?
> Biff: (Quavering) I'm nothing, Pop. Can't you understand that? There's no spite in it any more. I'm just what I am, that's all! (R, p. 2-80)

The earlier version did not serve Miller's thematic purpose. If Biff is to represent a hopeful alternative to the crushing law of success, he must have gotten beyond the tortured emotions and the moral confusion of the Loman family. He must seem cooler, more gentle, and in charge as he moves in to replace Willy and his values at the end of the play. Miller's revisions accomplished this, and on the whole, conveyed Biff's character more subtly, but something of Biff's dramatic power and emotional immediacy was lost in the process.

Notes

[1] Arthur Miller, Introduction, *Arthur Miller's Collected Plays* (New York: Viking, 1957), I, p. 36. All further references to this work will appear in the text.
[2] Arthur Miller, "The *Salesman* Has a Birthday" in *The Theater Essays of Arthur Miller*, ed. Robert A. Martin (New York: Penguin, 1978), p. 14.

[3] Arthur Miller, *Death of a Salesman* (New York: Viking, 1949), p. 133. All further references to this work will appear in the text.

[4] Arthur Miller, *Death of a Salesman*, TCCMS/Final Script, with Revisions and AMS by Miller on first page. This and all other unpublished versions of *Salesman* cited are in the Harry Ransom Humanities Research Center, University of Texas at Austin. All further references to this manuscript will appear in the text and will be cited as R.

[5] See Arthur Miller, *Timebends: A Life* (New York: Grove, 1987), p. 189. Here Miller offers one explanation for his revision of the restaurant scene:

> My one scary hour came with the climactic restaurant fight between Willy and the boys, when it all threatened to come apart. I had written a scene in which Biff resolves to tell Willy that the former boss from whom Biff had planned to borrow money to start a business has refused to so much as see him and does not even remember his working for the firm years ago. But on meeting his brother and father in the restaurant, he realizes that Willy's psychological stress will not permit the whole catastrophic truth to be told and he begins to trim the bad news. From moment to moment the scene as originally written had so many shadings of veracity that Arthur Kennedy, a very intelligent citizen indeed, had trouble shifting from a truth to a half-truth to a fragment of truth and back to the whole truth, all of it expressed in quickly delivered, very short lines. The three actors, with Kazan standing beside them, must have repeated the scene through a whole working day, and it still wobbled. "I don't see how we can make it happen," Kazan said as we left the theatre that evening. "Maybe you ought to try simplifying it for them." I went home and worked through the night and brought in a new scene, which played much better and became the scene as finally performed.

Salesman:
Private Tensions Raised to a Poetic-Social Level

Janet Balakian

The form of *Salesman* suits its matter, and it responds to the paradox that Miller sees underlying the struggle taking place in modern drama: "a struggle at one and the same time to write of private persons privately and yet lift up their means of expression to a poetic--that is, a social--level."[1] To put it another way, Miller has chosen to write *Salesman* as an "inside of the head" play in order to reveal the profound impact that the world outside has on an individual psyche, how a culture shapes and breaks a human spirit. As he says in his essay "The Shadow of the Gods,"

> the hidden laws of fate lurked not only in the characters of people, but equally if not more imperiously in the world beyond the family parlor. Out there were the big gods, the ones whose disfavor could turn a proud and prosperous and dignified man into a frightened shell of a man whatever he thought of himself, and whatever he decided or didn't decide to do.[2]

Salesman depicts the collapse of an American myth through Willy Loman's mind, and it grapples with the moral, ethical, and social issues that characterize expressionistic plays: Strindberg's *The Dance of Death*, many of the plays of Wedekind, Georg Kaiser, and Ernst Toller in Germany, along with Karel Capek in Czechoslovakia. Of course, this European tradition found its way to America in O'Neill's *The Hairy Ape* and *The Emperor Jones*, and in Elmer Rice's *The Adding Machine*, whose Mr. Zero in some ways prefigures the Willy Loman predicament. But Miller's breed of expressionism differs from that of his American predecessors. *Salesman* is a "confessional play," and this form expresses Miller's larger end--the impact of "society" on the psyche as "a power and a mystery of custom . . . inside the man and surrounding him, as the fish is in the sea and the sea inside the fish, his birthplace and burial ground, promise and threat."[3] As he has said recently, "the play could reflect what I had always sensed as the unbroken tissue that was man and society, a single unit rather than two."[4]

Clearly, this is Miller's canonical concern. Since *The Man Who Had All the Luck* (1944), Miller has been absorbed with the tension between the given and the willed. He has told me, for example, that *The Ride Down Mount Morgan* asserts that "while we are weak the rules of life are powerful, and they exist. And that's a tragic view, and therefore hopeful."[5] The expressionistic setting of *Salesman* embodies this tragic view forty years earlier: a solid vault of apartment houses around the fragile, skeletal home symbolizes the encroachment of an urban economy on the home where "an air of the dream clings."[6] Miller defines the technique as follows: "the stage is stripped of knicknacks; instead it reveals symbolic *designs* which function as overt pointers toward the moral to be drawn from the action."[7] Thus, the expressionistic techniques--the use of typical personae, a symbolic setting, the fluidity of time--lend a mythic element to the play. The Loman house is as suffocated, as blocked in by "bricks and windows, windows and bricks" (*Salesman*, p. 17), as is each family member. And the sound of the flute crystallizes the collision between urban and rural: "*a melody is heard, played upon a flute . . . telling of grass and trees and the horizon*" (*Salesman*, p. 11). This pastoral melody is juxtaposed with those angular apartment houses. Moreover, "*the blue light of the sky falls upon the house and forestage*" while "*the surrounding area shows an angry glow of orange*" (*Salesman*, p. 11). These expressive details reflect Willy's deep sense of deracination as he complains that "the street is lined with cars. There's not a breath of fresh air in the neighborhood. The grass don't grow anymore, you can't raise a carrot in the backyard" (*Salesman*, p. 17).

The Lomans are confined and defined by their industrial world. Willy tries to compensate for this lost pastoralism and to retrieve the moment in history when one could forge one's identity with his own hands, by building the front stoop, putting up the ceiling in his home, planting a garden. He cannot make flutes and sell them on the frontier as his father did, so he tries to create his own frontier in the midst of his Brooklyn suburb. As Miller says, "Willy Loman is trying to write his name in a cake of ice on a hot July day" because what he does lacks any sense of permanence: Charley says in the Requiem, "for a salesman, there is no rock bottom to the life. He don't put a bolt to a nut, he don't tell you the law or give you medicine. He's a man way out there in the blue, riding on a smile and a shoeshine . . ." (*Salesman*, p. 138). Willy reflects the anxieties of a culture, which, as C.W.E. Bigsby states, exchanged a world of physical and moral possibility for the determinisms of modern commercial and industrial life, the country for the city. The dislocations of his private life are those of a society chasing material success. In short, this is Miller's requiem for a country with all the wrong dreams.[8]

The problem, of course, is that Willy believes in the myth of his community, and in an effort to make the myth work, he ignorantly sacrifices himself. Not only has the myth caused Willy to perceive himself as an outcast in life, but Miller also depicts him as such in death. In the "Requiem," the sacred ritual of the funeral is broken because only Willy's family, Charley, and Bernard attend. *Salesman*, then, is finally about the absence of ritual, of community and, therefore, of a religious world that has no place in Miller's entirely secular dramatic world. Ultimately, there is no audience for Willy, and the empty ritual of the funeral is emblematic of the community whose myth kills him. Unlike John Proctor who refuses to allow his community to violate his sense of self, and unlike Eddie Carbone who betrays his Sicilian community, Willy allows his community to betray himself.

The Dave Singleman myth has shaped Willy and he cannot reconcile himself to the fact that it is myth and no longer reality. If he had not met Singleman, he would have gone north with Ben. Willy explains the motivation that kept him from journeying with his brother when he asks: "what could be more satisfying than to be able to go, at the age of eighty-four, into twenty or thirty different cities, and pick up a phone, and be remembered and loved and helped by so many different people?" (*Salesman*, p. 81). He never realized, however, that Howard Wagner would replace Dave Singleman, supplanting "respect, and comradeship, and gratitude" (*Salesman*, p. 81) with heartless capitalism. Willy is as much a victim of Howard as he is of the tape recorder that he cannot control. Promises no longer matter, only profit.

Miller's use of expressionistic lighting points to Willy's lamentation for the world that died with Howard's father. Miller notes: "when Willy speaks to the chair where his former boss once sat, the chair emanated light, confirming the fact that 'we had moved inside Willy's system of loss, seeing the world as he saw it'" (*Timebends*, p. 189). His perception is ours--a human being has become an empty chair, and like Roslyn in *The Misfits*, who asks Gay, "what is there that stays?," Willy finds his world crumbling beneath his feet. Even Howard's language conveys his degradation of Willy: "If I had a spot, I'd slam you right in . . . it's a business, kid, and everybody's gotta pull his own weight" (*Salesman*, p. 80).

Miller, however, claims that *Salesman* is not attacking capitalism; the most humane character in the play is himself a capitalist. He insists that a play cannot be equated with a political philosophy, that it must be seen as a writer's total perception. As in *All My Sons*, he presents a humanized capitalism. Bigsby takes issue with Miller, claiming that in giving Willy charity, Charley does not threaten the structure that has exploited Willy. In fact, he underwrites the system that destroys him (*American Drama*, p. 183). But while Charley can move according to the way of the world and tries to tell Willy what the rules are--"You named him Howard, but you can't sell that," and while he says "my salvation is that I never took any interest in anything" (*Salesman*, pp. 97, 96)--he aches for Willy, gives him money, and cautions him against suicide, unlike Ben.

Predictably, the Chinese had difficulty understanding the ambiguity with which Miller presents capitalism precisely because of Charley. They saw the play as advocating capitalism: "if a man can have reached Willy's standard of living and still feel in bad straits, it can't be such as awful a system as is sometimes advertised."[9] When the play first appeared in America, it was attacked as a piece of Communist propaganda. And when the first film version was made, the producing company was so frightened that it produced a documentary film demonstrating how exceptional Willy Loman was, how necessary selling is to the economy, how secure a salesman's life really is, and how idiotic Miller's film was.

Yet the film industry was marketing the same illusion that Willy buys. Willy breaks down because the values that have shaped him break: "It's who you know and the smile on your face! It's contacts"; "Be liked and you will never want," he assures himself as well as his sons (*Salesman*, pp. 86, 33). He believes that appearances matter, and when they do not result in success he is baffled: "In the greatest country in the world a young man with such-- personal attractiveness, gets lost" (*Salesman*, p. 16). For Willy, "making the grade," being "well liked," playing ball, having dates, doing whatever it takes to get ahead--whether it is lying like Hap, or stealing like Biff--playing tennis "with fine people," walking into the jungle and coming out rich, knowing what one wants and going out to get it--all these derive from an American ethos that has instilled these values in him. His language is full of its cliches: "The world is an oyster, but you don't crack it open on a mattress"; "Knocked 'em cold in Providence, slaughtered 'em in Boston"; "We have quite a streak of self-reliance in our family"; Ben "started with the clothes on his back and ended up with diamond mines"; "A man who can't handle tools is not a man" (*Salesman*, pp. 41, 33, 81, 41, 44). Willy's ideas derive from classical Hobbesian liberalism that glorifies the individual and sees life as a Darwinian race. His emphasis on rugged individualism also has its roots in the Horatio Alger myth and in Ben Franklin's notions of industriousness as the means to success. Like the Alger character, Willy believes in the potential greatness of the common man, in the pursuit of money as the pursuit of happiness. Concerned about Biff's lack of direction and career at thirty-four, he tries to reassure himself that "Certain men just don't get started till later in life. Like Thomas Edison . . . Or B.F. Goodrich" (*Salesman*, p. 18). And this eternal hope is also characteristically American. In conversation, Miller has said that the belief in our perfectibility, in the idea that there is a natural order in favor of us, is uniquely American. Moreover, it "forms a context of irony for the kind of stories we generally tell each other," the greatest of which are of failure.[10] Clearly, this irony informs *Salesman* in that Willy's beliefs cause his calamity and his family's.

Happy has adopted Willy's values, and he exemplifies their vacuousness: "All I can do now is wait for the merchandise manager to die" (*Salesman*, p. 23). Like the manager, he will build house after house on Long Island without taking the time to live in them. "I don't know what the hell I'm workin' for," Hap tells his brother. "Sometimes I sit in my apartment--all alone. And I think of the rent I'm paying. And it's crazy" (*Salesman*, p. 23). And yet he wants to carry out Willy's dream, because "it's the only dream you can have--to come out number one man" (*Salesman*, p. 139). He is the half of Willy who kills himself for this dream. Hap anticipates the decadent capitalist, Ruggieri, in Miller's more recent play, *Clara*. They chase the world of appearances as Willy does: "Bernard can get the best marks in school, but when he gets out in the business world you'll be five times ahead of him. That's why I thank Almighty God you're both built like Adonises . . ." (*Salesman*, p. 33). Yet the Bernard that Willy mocks proves his myth about success incorrect. Without being rugged, athletic and well-liked, without lying, stealing, or throwing the long pass, Bernard becomes the prestigious lawyer, arguing a case before the Supreme Court, the one whom Willy asks for advice. Indeed, Bernard validates the dreams Willy had for Biff, but the means by which he attains them are light years from the way Willy believes they are secured.

In addition, the family in *Salesman* becomes the icon for an American myth, for an ideal that seems shattered beyond repair. When he directed the play in Beijing in 1983, Miller explained to the Chinese that the play is "really a love story between a man and his son, and in a crazy way between both and America" (*Beijing*, p. 46). He later added that he "allowed the love to be severed by anger" (*Beijing*, p. 177). The father-son conflict is the core of the play as it is through much of the Miller canon. Biff must protest against Willy and against the system he represents. It is interesting to note that the Chinese actor playing Biff assumed that Biff's rebellion was part of a larger anti-establishment movement, and Miller had to explain that the sixties had not happened yet, that Biff's rebellion is a personal one. Although personal, the rebellion is at once familial and societal because Miller's point is that the two are inextricably connected. In his notebook for *Salesman* he wrote himself the following memo:

> *Discover* . . . the link between Biff's work views and his anti W feelings. . . . How it happens that W's life is in Biff's hands--aside from Biff succeeding. There is W's guilt to Biff in re: The Woman . . . There is Biff's disdain for W's character, his false aims, his fictions, and these Biff cannot finally give up or alter. (Bigsby, *American Drama*, p. 176)

In fact, the private and public conflict become one. Biff, the poet, the other half of Willy and a predecessor to Victor in *The Price*, tells Hap, "we weren't brought up to grub for money" (*Salesman*, p. 24). He embodies the frontier spirit that Willy denies in himself by being a salesman: ". . . it's a measley manner of existence. . . . To devote your whole life to keeping stock, or making phone calls, or selling, or buying . . . when all you really desire is to be outdoors, with your shirt off. And always to have to get ahead of the next fella" (*Salesman*, p. 22). Like Bert in *A Memory of Two Mondays*, Biff must leave the warehouse and go on the road. And yet Biff comes running home because he feels he is getting nowhere "playing around with horses" (*Salesman*, p. 22). Miller explains:

> away from home Biff sometimes feels a painfully unrequited love for his father, a sense of something unfinished between them. . . . It's like needing somebody's blessing before you can enjoy doing a certain thing . . . your love for him blinds you; but you want it to free you to be your own man. . . . (*Beijing*, p. 79)

In his notes, Miller saw the conflict in Biff between his hatred for Willy and his own desire for success in New York as crucial to an understanding of the play. Equally important was the combination of guilt (of failure), hate, and love--all of which Willy hopes to resolve "by 'accomplishing' a 20,000 dollar death" (Bigsby, *American Drama*, p. 177).

Miller also wrote in his notes that Biff "has returned home resolved to disillusion W Forever, to set him upon a new path, and thus release him-self from responsibility for W . . ." (Bigsby, *American Drama*, p. 179). Biff ultimately unveils Willy's illusion for himself [Biff], but not for Willy. While Biff "lights out for territory ahead of the rest," a bit like Huck Finn, Willy dies to sustain his false dream. Nevertheless, as Miller says,

> love, which is in a race for Willy's faith, counters the law which says that a failure in society and in business has no right to live. But by the time Willy can perceive Biff's love it can serve only as an ironic comment upon the life he sacrificed for power and for success and its tokens.[11]

Even Linda's love for Willy cannot save him. While she knows that "attention must be paid" to Willy, that "a terrible thing is happening to him" (*Salesman*, p. 56), she does not understand that "Willy seeks an ecstasy, which the machine civilization deprives him."[12] When Willy returns home in the beginning of the play to say, "I couldn't make it" (*Salesman*, p. 13), Linda attributes his problem to the coffee, to the steeiing, to his glasses. In the Requiem she can only say, "He only needed a little salary" (*Salesman*, p. 137).

For Miller, all great plays must ask how one can make of the outside world a home,[13] and this is the problem of *Salesman*. Estranged by a myth and by overbearing economic forces, "the shadow of the gods," Willy Loman believes he can find a home only in death.

Some critics argue that Miller has written a play within a play, and that the social play is in the outer frame while the private illumination is in the inner one. The private and public conflicts, however, are one and the same, which is why the play takes the form of an exploration of Willy's mind. Miller argues that Willy is tragic because Willy knows something is profoundly wrong with the world in which he lives and he struggles to gain his rightful position, his personal dignity. As Miller puts it, Willy "is looking for his immortal soul."[14] If he had no values and ideals, he would be perfectly at home in his world. Like Eddie Carbone in *A View from the Bridge*, Willy "cannot settle for half" and "must pursue his dream of himself to the end."[15] In this sense, he exemplifies the single most powerful influence on Miller's early writing: "not only to depict why a man does what he does, or why he nearly didn't do it, but why he cannot simply walk away and say to hell with it. . . ."[16] Miller asserts that "the less capable a man is of walking away from the central conflict of the play, the closer he approaches a tragic existence."[17] He insists that Willy does not lack the perception of the false values to which he has committed himself, but rather he lacks the ability to articulate that awareness: "had Willy been unaware of his separation from values that endure he would have died contentedly while polishing his car, probably on a Sunday afternoon with the ball game coming over the radio."[18] But if he is aware of his separation from values that endure, then why does he kill himself for those hollow values? What Miller says about Willy and what Willy actually does in the play do not entirely coincide.

In discovering the form for *Salesman*, Miller was as obsessed as the character he created:

> I was obsessed these days by vague but exciting images of what can only be called a trajectory, an arched flow of storytelling with neither transitional dialogue nor a single fixed locale, a mode that would open a man's head for a play to take place inside it, evolving through concurrent rather than consecutive actions . . . dialogue that would simply leap from bone to bone of a skeleton that would not for an instant cease being added to, an organism as strictly economic as a leaf, as trim as an ant . . . a play that would cut through time like a knife through a layer cake or a road through a mountain revealing its geologic layers, and instead of one incident in one time-frame succeeding another, display past and present concurrently, with neither one ever coming to a stop. (*Timebends*, pp. 129-31)

Salesman cuts through time because its concern is not to create an exposition, climax, and denouement, but rather to expose the consciousness of a man that has been formed by his society. Significantly, this method that attracted Miller in 1949 informs his play of 1986, *Clara*, which is governed by "a kind of imploding of time--moments when a buried layer of experience suddenly surges upward to become the new surface of one's attention. . ." (*Timebends*, p. 590). In the new play, however, Kroll has great difficulty remembering the past when he instilled the liberal values in his daughter that led to her death. In *Salesman*, Willy cannot forget the past, and his mental breakdown discloses the impact of social laws--those "shadows of the gods"--on the individual psyche.

The importance of economic forces to Miller is evident by the fact that he had originally toyed with the title *A Period of Grace* for *Salesman* (Bigsby, *American Drama*, p. 185). Such a title would have accentuated Willy's preoccupation with overdue insurance payments and his fear of being swallowed up by the system. This is a concern that led Miller in the seventies to write and rewrite his play about the Depression, *The American Clock*. The epic theatricalism of that play depicts America talking to itself about the meaning of the Crash, unlike *Salesman* in which America speaks through Willy's consciousness.

Altogether, Miller's canonical concern with social forces has led him to explore a variety of dramatic forms. He has always felt an affinity to the Greeks and to the German expressionists, both of whom are interested in presenting hidden forces rather than the particulars of a character. In *Salesman*, society has become what the Gods were for the Greeks: the force that shapes human destiny. Not only has Miller raised the private to the social or poetic in *Salesman*, but he has also created a new form. Lee J. Cobb was right when he told Miller in Kermit Bloomgarden's office a week before rehearsals began, "this play is a watershed. The American theatre will never be the same" (*Timebends*, p. 187). In its way of bending time, its neglect of transitional scenes, in its portrait of a psychological process as a collecting point for all that Willy Loman's life in society has poured into him, *Salesman* was a "time bomb under American capitalism" that exposed the psyche of American culture (*Timebends*, p. 184).

Notes

[1] Arthur Miller, "On Social Plays" in *The Theater Essays of Arthur Miller*, ed. Robert A. Martin (New York: Penguin, 1978), p. 57.
[2] Arthur Miller, "The Shadows of the Gods" in *The Theater Essays of Arthur Miller*, p. 178.
[3] Arthur Miller, "Introduction to the *Collected Plays*" in *The Theater Essays of Arthur Miller*, p. 143.

⁴ Arthur Miller, *Timebends: A Life* (New York: Grove, 1987), p. 182. All further references to this work will appear in the text.

⁵ Author's Conversation with Arthur Miller, June 1989.

⁶ Arthur Miller, *Death of a Salesman* (New York: Penguin, 1976), p. 11. All further references to this work will appear in the text.

⁷ Arthur Miller, "The Family in Modern Drama" in *The Theater Essays of Arthur Miller*, p. 74.

⁸ C. W. E. Bigsby, *Twentieth-Century American Drama* (Cambridge: Cambridge University Press, 1984), II, p. 186. All further references to this work will appear in the text.

⁹ Arthur Miller, *Salesman in Beijing* (New York: Viking, 1984), p. 86. All further references to this work will appear in the text.

¹⁰ Arthur Miller, as quoted in Matthew C. Roudané, "An Interview with Arthur Miller" in *Conversations with Arthur Miller*, ed. Matthew C. Roudané (Jackson: University Press of Mississippi, 1987), p. 361.

¹¹ Arthur Miller, "Introduction to the *Collected Plays*" in *The Theater Essays of Arthur Miller*, p. 149.

¹² Arthur Miller, in interview with Phillip Gelb, "Morality and Modern Drama" in *The Theater Essays of Arthur Miller*, p. 195.

¹³ Arthur Miller, "The Family in Modern Drama" in *The Theater Essays of Arthur Miller*, p. 73.

¹⁴ Arthur Miller, in interview with Phillip Gelb, "Morality and Modern Drama" in *The Theater Essays of Arthur Miller*, p. 198.

¹⁵ Arthur Miller, "Introduction to the *Collected Plays*" in *The Theater Essays of Arthur Miller*, p. 148.

¹⁶ Arthur Miller, "Introduction to the *Collected Plays*" in *The Theater Essays of Arthur Miller*, p. 117.

¹⁷ Arthur Miller, "Introduction to the *Collected Plays*" in *The Theater Essays of Arthur Miller*, p. 118.

¹⁸ Arthur Miller, "Introduction to the *Collected Plays*" in *The Theater Essays of Arthur Miller*, p. 148.

Is This a Play About Women?:
A Feminist Reading of *Death of a Salesman*

Charlotte Canning

At first glance *Death of a Salesman* is not a promising text for the feminist reader. The play is ostensibly concerned with Willy Loman's struggle between his dreams and his reality and how that struggle is played out through and by the next generation of men, his sons. The over-determined presence of men and the blanket absence of women implies that this text holds nothing for either the feminist reader or someone wishing to apply feminist theory. However, as Sue-Ellen Case points out in the introduction to *Feminism and Theater*, another perspective is possible: "I debated whether or not to begin this book with works by men, but finally decided that many of us originally adopted feminism because of the pain and anger we felt when we encountered the prejudices and omissions of the traditional theater."[1] Beginning where many feminists began, with the works of men, can be a productive start or reminder, especially if one does not have a familiarity with feminist theory or a negative conception of it as shaped by mainstream conservative thought. As long as plays like *Salesman* uncritically occupy prominent and visible places in the literary and production canons there can be no argument about post-feminism or the irrelevance of feminist readings. Feminists might note that despite its concentration on the father/son dyad, *Death of a Salesman* is not devoid of women and, in fact, they play an extremely crucial role in shaping the action and ideas of the text.

Having said that the play has potential for a feminist reading there is still the question of how that reading would be performed. As already stated, the text upon initial examination appears to be a poor choice. However, with a closer look some reading strategies quickly present themselves. A feminist reader could approach the text with deconstructive strategies and examine *Death of a Salesman* for its treatment of women and reveal the sexism in its construction. Another approach might see the play as a reflection of social gender construction and demonstrate how the codes and norms that bind Linda are just as damaging to Willy, Biff, and Happy. The play could also be critiqued formally, discussing the effects of realism on the creation of female characters. Or, finally, the feminist reader could decide that this play offers nothing and abandon it entirely. While this last option seems tempting, the complete rejection of works that are deemed sexist or demeaning to women is not an entirely practical, feasible, or even desirable option.

Reading *Death of a Salesman* through a feminist lens raises the question of canon formation and perpetuation within the institutions of literature and theater. Using the play to produce a feminist reading could be seen as complicity with a sexist system that erases the work of women or as an appropriative move on the part of institutions to deny or negate the oppositional power of feminism. This legitimate concern can be met by concomitant readings of works by women and a conscious acknowledgment of the issue. It is important to remember that feminism is not just another theoretical apparatus for reading a text, but a political position adopted by women in order to oppose and change the oppression they experience in their daily lives. In order to maintain an awareness of this, the feminist reader must construct a conscious framework for her reading, because unlike work "on patriarchal playwrights working within a traditional theater," there is no feminist "context for a critical treatment . . . 'always already' securely in place."[2] In other words, the context for a feminist reception of *Death of a Salesman* does not exist and must be continuously created.

This still does not answer the charge that reading this play is just a clever way to avoid reading other, less canonical, texts. The answer to this charge lies in the context and content of other readings. If the reader goes on to encounter a variety of works across the boundaries of race, ethnicity, gender, and sexuality, then the reading of *Death of a Salesman* is not particularly remarkable. But if the reader does not immerse herself in a diversity of material by reading and attending other plays, then it might well be that a feminist approach to this play is a way to avoid reading feminist works themselves.

More practically, to imagine that canonical works like *Death of a Salesman* will cease to be read or produced is ingenuous and disregards theater history, if nothing else. This play occupies an important place in American theater history and readers and spectators should have a familiarity with all works that have played a crucial role in shaping the United States theater scene. This in no way mitigates the arguments and responsibilities that the works one reads or produces should include material from outside mainstream tradition, often defined by and limited to texts by white men, but this approach does suggest that plays like *Death of a Salesman* can co-exist with feminist works, plays by people of color, and texts from outside the western theater tradition. Feminist criticism "has contributed significantly to displacing the complacency that, until recently, assumed that the literary canon was closed."³ The most productive way into the play might be through a combination of the above-mentioned approaches, those that seek to deconstruct the play and provide a context for it while simultaneously finding productive and constructive ways to view and produce *Death of a Salesman*.

One of the most important elements of reading this or any other play is to remain aware that it is a performance text, not a literary one, and that the words read were meant to be heard and enacted. Too often plays are not read as potential performances but as works of literature. In order to escape this, *Death of a Salesman* could be approached through feminist theory as potential for a production concept. This method would reinforce the idea that it was indeed created to be performed, not read. Thus, this paper will explore specific strategies for creating a feminist framework through which to read *Death of a Salesman*.

In the introduction to volume one of *The Collected Plays of Arthur Miller*, the playwright offers his thoughts and reflections on the collection that represents ten years of his work. The plays, he states, were his response to the constantly changing society around him. Attempting to tell truths that would lessen the isolation of individuals, he sought to demonstrate that many of the problems or anxieties believed by people to be unique are shared with others. Thus Miller frames his plays as moments of truth and his method as a distillation of what already exists. He writes:

> These plays, in a sense, are my response to what was "in the air," they are one man's way of saying to his fellow men, "This is what you see everyday, or think or feel; now I will show you what you really know but have not had the time, or the disinterestedness, or the insight, or the information to understand consciously."⁴

Implied in this quotation is that what is in his plays is just that which is natural and inevitable. He conveniently erases his role as creator and instead positions himself as a cultural translator who is only presenting the public with its own view of society.

Miller perceives himself as simply performing Shakespeare's definition of theater as a mirror held up to nature. However, this description is not entirely satisfactory, especially for a feminist reader out to demonstrate that the female characters in *Death of a Salesman* are not real women but male constructions of women as men would like them to be. In the play everything is learned about how men position women, but nothing about women and how they perceive the world. As Jill Dolan has pointed out about how a feminist might view the theater-as-mirror analogy: "Attention has shifted from the mirror's image to the mirror's surface and frame. By calling the entire device into question, doubt has been cast on the accuracy of the image it reflects."[5] For, as Dolan explains, the hands that hold the mirror control what it reflects and "the hands holding the mirror up to nature have not been our own."[6] Miller's claim that he has just reproduced what is "in the air" is naive and obfuscating. He has created a play derived from mainstream notions of women, heterosexual relationships, and gender definition, but this does not mean that they accurately represent the experiences of everyone in society. In a subsequent interview Miller again stressed that he was merely reproducing a truthful picture of reality. The women characters in his plays, he commented, "are *of necessity* auxiliaries to that action, which is carried by the male characters."[7] This statement raises some questions. Why is it necessary for women to be "auxiliaries" to the action? What purpose does that role for them serve? These questions are the beginnings of feminist theory. Questions about the ways in which material women are treated or women characters are constructed are the same questions that feminist theorists have asked themselves since they began to build a body of feminist theory.

Traditional analyses have focussed on Willy, Biff, and Happy.[8] The women characters are usually viewed as ancillary to the main action or as necessary plot devices. However, even a superficial skimming of the text reveals that women either play a crucial role in almost every scene or form a significant part of the men's conversation. The overt "male-ness" of the play does make it easily possible for readers to "overlook, patronize, or devalue the significance of women in the play."[9] But a close examination of the three male protagonists reveals that women are not marginalized figures.

Biff and Happy can only define themselves in relation to women. The significant change in Biff's approach to life, as measured by the loss of respect and esteem he once held for his father, stems from finding Willy in a hotel room with The Woman. Before this occurs Biff was popular with the girls at school, as Happy boasts about his brother: "There's a crowd of girls behind him every time classes change."[10] However, after witnessing his father's adultery, Biff alters his relations with women. He shows little interest in them, perhaps to the point of fearing them. When Biff reminds Happy that Biff taught him everything he knows about women, Happy admits that he is still shy of women. Biff does not believe him and Happy counters: "I think I got less bashful and you got more so. What happened, Biff? Where's the old humor, the old confidence?" (*Salesman*, p. 137). For Happy, women are defining in an entirely different way. While Biff no longer seems to want to have anything to do with women, Happy has become a womanizer. He tells his brother: "I can get that anytime I want, Biff. Whenever I feel disgusted. The only trouble is, it gets like bowling or something. I just keep knocking them over and it doesn't mean anything" (*Salesman*, p. 140). Women are merely objects to be obtained or rejected. As Happy goes on to describe his most recent date, he reveals that he uses women to relieve his sense of inadequacy and express his jealousy for men who are more successful than he is:

> I don't know what gets into me, maybe I just have an overdeveloped sense of competition or something, but I went and ruined her, and furthermore I just can't get rid of her. And he's the third executive I've done that to. Isn't that a crummy characteristic? And to top it all, I go to their weddings. (*Salesman*, p. 141)

Happy can only perceive women as property and a way to express his superiority over the supervisors at his job where he is unable to get ahead.

For Biff, women represent his father's betrayal of the family. For Happy, says Kay Stanton, they are "scapegoats for his inability to marry" ("American Dream," p. 74). In this sense women are crucial both to the dramatic action of the play and to the ideas that underlie and support it. Through women, men express who they are and how they define themselves. Miller has created a world where women passively allow men to enact their fantasies and needs out across women's bodies. The exchange of women among the men and the women's representation as objects to be exchanged, "eliminates women as active subjects in the play."[11] The women are shaped by a man's imagination and defined by male needs. Women are, as Happy says to Stanley, "strudel" (*Salesman*, p. 194).

Miller has used women definitively for Willy's character as well. The most obvious example is that Linda is created as a foil for Willy's dreams, hopes, and ambitions. Her sole purpose is to support and nurture him, even when he mistreats or abuses her. The opening stage directions assert:

> *[S]he has developed an iron repression of her exceptions to Willy's behavior--she more than loves him, she admires him, as though his mercurial nature, his temper, his massive dreams and little cruelties, served her only as sharp reminders of the turbulent longings within him, longings which she shares but lacks the temperament to utter and follow to their end. (Salesman, p. 131)*

Miller has created the ultimate wife: loyal, unselfish, and forgiving, a nineteenth-century "angel in the house." Linda never voices criticism of Willy even when he lies to her about his commissions, mocks her suggestions, or orders her from the room. Linda is the perfect fantasy wife. In response to criticism that Linda is too passive, Miller asserted: "When I directed *Salesman* in China I had Linda 'in action. . . .' She's got the vital information all the time. Linda sustains the illusion because that's the only way Willy can be sustained. . . ." (*Conversations*, p. 370). But Miller skillfully elides the fact that her actions are never assertive or productive. They are actions of a male fantasy--a woman whose entire efforts are devoted to *his* ends, *his* needs.

Interestingly, some critics feel that because Linda works so hard to sustain Willy's illusions it is she who is responsible for his struggle and his problems.[12] This is indicative of the problem of the character. While Willy admits to Linda in a moment of tenderness that she is his "foundation and support" (*Salesman*, p. 135), she is also the ground upon which he asserts his control and desire, things he cannot do in the business world. It is impossible to imagine Willy without Linda and Linda without Willy because she is the only woman he can feel successful with, the woman he can exploit. As Kay Stanton has pointed out, in this play success is "bound up with the sexual exploitation of women" ("American Dream," p. 73). On the road Willy had Miss Francis to make him feel important and liked; at home he has Linda.

To see how a feminist analysis develops, it is important to stress that these characters are not people, but textual creations. Linda does not admire Willy because he is a great hero, but because Miller needed a character who made Willy's potential clear. Without her most famous speech where she asserts that "attention must be paid" (*Salesman*, p. 162), Willy would be indistinguishable from anyone else who has been unable to achieve his dreams. According to Stanton, Linda is "the foundation that has allowed the Loman men to build themselves up, if only in dreams, and she is the support that enables them to continue despite their failures" ("American Dream," p. 75). The other women serve similar, if less central, functions. Miss Francis/The Woman is an expression of Willy's need to be liked and the hypocrisy underlying his rhetoric, Miss Forsythe embodies Happy's assertion that women are essentially unfaithful and "on call" (*Salesman*, p. 196), and even Charley's secretary Jenny is suspect; Willy asks her "Workin'? Or still honest?" (*Salesman*, p. 187). The only roles for women are whores or mothers and both are necessary to the men in the play.

Before writing *Death of a Salesman*, Miller described his need to construct the building within which the play would be written. Noting that despite the fact that "a pair of carpenters could have put [it] up . . . in two days at most," he states that he experienced an inexplicable need to do it himself no matter how long it took.[13] When he completed the building, he described his sense of satisfaction as a feeling of having "mastered the rain and cooled the sun" (*Timebends*, p. 183). From that moment of "mastery" and domination came *Death of a Salesman*. Cast by Miller himself as a heroic and singular effort, the play could be read as the product of a single genius. Contrast this then with Elia Kazan's depiction in his autobiography of the initial moments of the production process. He describes the script he received as "a play waiting for a directorial solution."[14] According to Kazan, Miller wrote in the initial stage directions that Willy enters and fits his key into an "invisible door," and it was Jo Meilziner, the scenic designer, who offered the "concept of a house standing like a spectre behind all the scenes of the play, always present as it might always be present in Willy's mind. . ." (*A Life*, p. 361). Kazan forthrightly admits that he and Miller often received praise for what was Mielziner's idea. The stage directions at the beginning of the published version of the play describing the house came not from Miller, but from Mielziner's realization of the play for the production. Kazan commented:

> A published play is often the record of a collaboration. . . . The theater is not an exclusively literary form. Although the playscript is the essentially important element, after that is finished, actors, designers, directors, technicians "write" the play together. (*A Life*, p. 362)

This account differs widely from Miller's. Kazan positions Miller's efforts as a beginning, an initial foray; Miller sees his efforts as God-like, equating his work with conquest and domination.

For the feminist reader, Kazan's view may be the more promising one. Viewing it as collaboration creating a product shaped by the contributions of many different perspectives rather than the heroic effort of a single individual enables the reader to position *Salesman* more definitively as a text defined by material circumstances, as well as by intellectual, aesthetic, and political discourses. Miller's extra-textual description of domination could be equated with the intra-textual attempts to dominate women. The possibilities of theater, more specifically feminist theater, foreground alternate possibilities for reading and producing the play.

The argument outlined here demonstrates that *Death of a Salesman* can be used productively to articulate a feminist critique. This is but one kind of reading that might be performed on this play. It must also be kept in mind that the feminist reading performed here is necessarily incomplete. In order to gain a fuller understanding of the depth and range of feminist theory, one must also turn to more positive examples, that is, to works by women. Feminism is not simply a negative critique that foregrounds moments where women are objectified or victimized. Feminism and feminist theory are primarily concerned with the works of women and women's experiences and it is a far more complex body of theory than the reading performed here can possibly demonstrate. However, having offered that caveat, I would like to stress that reading *Death of a Salesman* with a feminist perspective is an important action and can only serve to bring the play to life in a new way for those encountering it for the first time or for the twentieth time.

Notes

[1] Sue-Ellen Case, *Feminism and Theater* (New York: Methuen, 1987), p. 1.

[2] Sue-Ellen Case, "Judy Grahn's Gynopoetics: *The Queen of Swords*," *Studies in the Literary Imagination*, 21, No. 2 (1988), 47.

[3] June Schlueter, ed., Introduction, *Feminist Rereadings of Modern American Drama* (Rutherford: Fairleigh Dickinson University Press, 1989), p. 11.

[4] Arthur Miller, Introduction, *Arthur Miller's Collected Plays* (New York: Viking Press, 1957), I, p. 11.

[5] Jill Dolan, "Gender Impersonation Onstage: Destroying or Maintaining the Mirror of Gender Roles?" *Women and Performance*, 4 (1985), 5.

[6] Jill Dolan, p. 5.

[7] Arthur Miller, as quoted in Matthew C. Roudané, "An Interview with Arthur Miller" in *Conversations with Arthur Miller*, ed. Matthew C. Roudané (Jackson: University Press of Mississippi, 1987), p. 370. All further references to this work will appear in the text as *Conversations*.

[8] See, for example, Dennis Welland, *Miller: The Playwright* (London: Methuen, 1983), p. 48. In his discussion of *Death of a Salesman*, Welland could be speaking for the majority of critics when he writes: "It is, of course, a play about a man and his sons. . . ."

[9] Kay Stanton, "Women and the American Dream of *Death of a Salesman*," *Feminist Rereadings of Modern American Drama*, p. 67. All further references to this work will appear in the text in the shortened form "American Dream."

[10] Arthur Miller, *Death of a Salesman*, in *Arthur Miller's Collected Plays*, I, p. 145. All further references to this play will appear in the text.

[11] Gayle Austin, "The Exchange of Women and Male Homosexual Desire in Arthur Miller's *Death of a Salesman* and Lillian Hellman's *Another Part of the Forest*," *Feminist Rereadings of Modern American Drama*, p. 61.

[12] In endnotes to her article "Women and the American Dream of *Death of a Salesman*," Kay Stanton documents the various critical attitudes people have taken toward Linda Loman. One critic describes "Linda's facility for prodding Willy to his doom" while another accuses her of "attempting to destroy her husband" (pp. 98-99). Given the circumstances of the play, it is interesting to observe the torturous routes critics will follow in order to absolve Willy of any responsibility for his own downfall.

[13] Arthur Miller, *Timebends: A Life* (New York: Grove, 1987), p. 183. All further references to this work will appear in the text.

[14] Elia Kazan, *A Life* (New York: Doubleday, 1989), p. 361. All further references to this work will appear in the text.

Miller's *Salesman:*
An Early Vision of Absurdist Theatre

Paula Langteau

Most discussions of Arthur Miller takes place within the context of his work as a conventional realist. As a result, critics, considering realism Miller's "mature style,"[1] have largely ignored his use of the techniques of the theatre of the absurd. Granted, some have identified so-called "experimental techniques" in Miller's drama, but these techniques have been considered only insofar as they depart from realism and not as they tend toward other dramatic forms, particularly the absurdist dramatic convention.[2] Additionally, some have examined one or more of these established techniques in Miller's drama but then outright rejected the possibility of a connection to their absurdist philosophical underpinnings.[3] And others have focused not on Miller's use of absurdist convention but rather on the statements he has made in opposition to the absurdist theatre.[4] Indeed, Miller himself long identified his work with realism, and it was not until his 1987 autobiography, *Timebends: A Life,* that he expressed an identification with the absurdist movement in theatre. He writes:

> In the early fifties the so-called theatre of the absurd was still in the offing, and I would resist most of its efforts as spurious, but each generation of writers has an investment in its accomplishments that it is obliged to defend. Had I really obeyed the logic of my daily observations, however, I would have been an absurdist myself, for most of the time I was shaking my head at what was going on and laughing the dry laugh of incredulous amazement.[5]

Unbeknownst perhaps to Miller, not only had he obeyed the logic of his daily observations and effectively blended "experimental" absurdist techniques into his realism, but he had done so *before* the early fifties, before absurdism was first recognized in the theatre.

According to Martin Esslin's *Theatre of the Absurd*, the groundbreaking work to first explain the convention and the one still recognized as the definitive study of the topic, absurdism is the theatrical portrayal of the irrational human condition, based on the existential philosophy of man's inability to find ultimate answers in an orderless world. But, what makes absurdism distinct from existential drama is its presentation on the stage. In the Theatre of the Absurd, the subject matter and the form in which it is expressed are integrated. The human condition is not just discussed; it is shown. As Esslin points out, while existentialism argues about the absurdity of the human condition, absurdism "merely *presents* it in being--that is, in terms of concrete stage images. . . ."[6] In *Death of a Salesman*, Miller presents concrete stage images that convey the absurdity of the human condition, the absurdity of man's endeavor to assemble meaning and establish personal identity through his struggle with the perceived expectations of his world.

Absurdist playwrights use different techniques to accomplish the same objective: to provide what Esslin describes as an image of "one individual human being's intuition of the ultimate realities as he experiences them; the fruits of one man's descent into the depths of his personality, his dreams, fantasies, and nightmares" (*Absurd*, p. 402). Esslin takes care to explain that the approach for each absurdist playwright is different: "Each has his own personal approach to both subject-matter and form; his own roots, sources, and background" (*Absurd*, p. 22). Therefore, no specific checklist of absurdist techniques can be compiled. However, an examination of the techniques used by established absurdist playwrights reveals that certain means are more effective at conveying an absurdist message. Whatever the techniques chosen by the playwright, together they form the absurdist poetic image, which may include elements that contribute to the perceptions of the subconscious as well as the visual elements of setting and performance. As Esslin describes it, the poetic image, using all the techniques of the drama, represents the "totality of perception" (*Absurd*, p. 406), and as Sandra Page Turney explains, because the elements work together simultaneously, they create "images that the audience can perceive and comprehend instantly, much in the same manner that one sees an abstract painting."[7]

Miller similarly describes how he was attempting to communicate in *Salesman*. In a letter, he explains that the play "came out of a vision of simultaneity in human thought-action-memory for which at the time there was no dramatic expression."[8] That vision might well be described as an absurdist poetic image. Further Miller uses numerous interrelated techniques to depict the futile struggle of his protagonist, Willy Loman. Of those techniques, I have identified six (though there may be more) from among those Esslin examines as successful absurdist methods.

The six theatrical techniques through which Miller conveys *Salesman's* poetic image, to be discussed here as distinct from one another, in truth cannot be separated in performance. They include: 1. the symbolic set, 2. the violation of the time sequence, 3. the dream quality of the play, 4. the use of non-rational events, 5. the devaluation of language, and 6. the cycle of the play.

Symbolic Set

One of the first goals in absurdist drama is to alienate the audience from the realism of the situation, causing them to directly confront the playwright's absurdist message. Esslin describes how Bertolt Brecht used non-realistic form to inhibit audience identification with the dramatized event, producing what he called the "alienation effect" (*Absurd*, p. 410). Similarly, Miller effectively distances his audience through his use of a symbolic set, reminding them that the play is not meant to present reality.

Envisioning the set during the composition of *Death of a Salesman*, Miller writes, in his Introduction to volume 1 of his *Collected Plays*, that he had imagined "an enormous face the height of the proscenium arch which would appear and then open up, and we would see the inside of a man's head."[9] Although Miller did not use this image for the set he finally put to print, the absurdist overtones are still conveyed in the final set. According to Enoch Brater, Miller's set immediately breaks down a sense of realism, "play[ing] a metaphorically supporting role."[10] The script describes it as "*wholly or, in some places, partially transparent,*"[11] conveying an emptiness or a dissection of reality. The salesman's house is surrounded by "*towering, angular shapes. . . . the surrounding area shows an angry glow of orange. . . . [And] we see a solid vault of apartment houses around the small, fragile-seeming house*" (*Salesman*, p. 11). Robert F. Whitman explains: "The setting, then, with its implacable, ominous apartments seemingly crushing the fragile, withering house beneath them . . . is a symbolic suggestion of what has happened, and is happening to, [Willy Loman]."[12] Further, the forward stage area serves more than one purpose, "*as the back yard as well as the locale of all Willy's imaginings and of his city scenes*" (*Salesman*, p. 12). Accessing the forestage, actors violate set boundaries, stepping through wall-lines during the scenes of the past. The symbolic set thereby removes the audience from the realism of the action, representing instead the flow of Willy's thought.

Violation of Time Sequence

Miller incorporates into his violation of set boundaries the violation of time sequence, through the intermingling of past and present. Ben's presence in Willy's present reality violates the convention of flashback used in realistic drama. Unlike conventional flashback, in which the character remembers an incident of the past and reacts to it in the present, *Salesman's* technique can best be described as a past-in-present experience, in which Willy's deceased brother addresses Willy's current situation. The past, embodied in Ben, directly bears upon the present, Willy's decision to take his life. Martin Erwin, commenting on Miller's use of blocks of past time in *Salesman*, writes: "the events of the past do not constitute an interruption of the present--they *are* the present."[13] Past and present are fused, and together they immediately impact the course of the play.

Likewise, theatre of the absurd stops the clock. Time becomes an extraneous detail, and without chronological sequence or some other structured time pattern, plot breaks down. Esther Merle Jackson notes that "*Death of a Salesman*, as a vision, follows an aesthetic, rather than a logical mode of development."[14] The protagonist is frozen in a moment of time in which the audience perceives the image of his predicament. In his autobiography, Miller, explaining the reasons for this presentation, states that for him, man "is his past at every moment and that the present is merely that which the past is capable of noticing and smelling and reacting to" (*Timebends*, p. 131). Thus, he explains, he created *Death of a Salesman* to be a play that "did not allow man to 'forget' and turned him to see present through past and past through present" (*Timebends*, p. 131). The boundaries of time become imperceptible, and the message of the play takes precedence over the sequence of action.

Dream Qualities

Since the audience experiences the play through the filter of Willy's mind, interchanging past and present, the action can be confusing, offering dreamlike perceptions of reality. Inside Willy's mind his thoughts are jumbled, contradictory and confused, to the point that he has difficulty concentrating even enough to drive his car (*Salesman*, p. 13). His mind cannot focus on the task at hand. He is troubled by "strange thoughts" that distract him from the present.

Similarly, he has difficulty distinguishing between the past and present, blending not only the separate two, but also separate past realities. In Act I, Willy experiences a past-in-present conversation with his wife, during which he immerses himself further into the past to continue the conversation with the Woman in Boston. Such double-absorption into the past takes the audience to a level of the subconscious inaccessible in purely realistic drama and suggests the extent to which Willy is losing touch with external reality. Again, in Act II, when Biff, in the restaurant scene, struggles to tell his father the truth about his traumatic visit to Oliver, Willy avoids confronting the unpleasant reality through a sudden interruption by the past: the script tells us, "*A single trumpet note jars the ear*" (*Salesman*, p. 109), and Willy is set off in a fury, wildly babbling about Biff's failing math in high school. Willy's muddled confusion reaches its peak when "*sounds, faces, voices seem to be swarming in upon his and he flicks at them, crying Sh! Sh!*" (*Salesman*, p. 136) just before he goes out to commit suicide.

Confused, trance-like thought is an element of absurdism. Esslin points out that "basic among the age-old traditions present in the Theatre of the Absurd is the use of . . . dreamlike modes of thought--the projection into concrete terms of psychological realities" (*Absurd*, pp. 348-49). Such a projection of psychological reality is what Miller provides for the audience with the visual presentation on stage of Willy's absorption into the past. While in the script Miller describes the play as "*a dream rising out of reality*" (*Salesman*, p. 11), it might well have been called reality rising out of a dream because Willy's psychological reality *becomes* the physical reality for both himself and the audience. In a world that is frightening and provides no security, Willy has retreated into the depths of his mind to bring out a reality of his own.

Non-Rational Events

Because Willy is dealing with two conflicting realities--external reality and his own psychological reality--his actions seem mechanical and lacking of logical motivation, particularly as he phases in and out of contact exclusively with the present reality. Following his first conversation with Ben in Act I, Willy, oblivious to Linda's protests, goes out of door in his slippers. After reliving the affair scene in Act II, he finds himself on the restaurant's washroom floor, and, late in the play, he begins planting a garden at night. Willy Loman, like Vladimir and Estragon in *Waiting for Godot* whose actions are subject to their illusion of Godot's impending arrival, behaves like many absurd characters, like "mechanical puppets" (*Absurd*, p. 22) subject to the non-rational motivating forces of their own confused minds.

Devaluation of Language

Further affected by Willy's shifts in reality is his speech, which becomes confused as his thoughts stray. In his psychological transitions to and from the past, he often babbles incoherently to the characters on stage with him in the present, a behavior characteristic of absurdist characters (*Absurd*, p. 22). In Act I, while playing cards with Charley, Willy carries on a conversation with Ben. When Charley questions what Willy is talking about, Willy becomes "*unnerved*" and takes out his confusion in anger against Charley (*Salesman*, p. 46). In a later incident, at the restaurant with his sons in the second act, Willy frightens the boys when he begins shouting in response to the voice of the operator, paging him in the past (*Salesman*, p. 111). The boys finally leave him in the restaurant washroom when his submersion in the past becomes too much of a public embarrassment.

Miller reduces the meaning of the dialogue not only through Willy's babblings, but also through the cliches created by Willy's repetitive recitation of phrases that help Willy maintain his hopeful illusion. In his mind, he hears Ben repeatedly proclaiming, "William, when I walked into the jungle, I was seventeen. When I walked out I was twenty-one. And, by God, I was rich!" (*Salesman*, p. 52). Willy also recites his own favorite key to success which suggests that one needs not just to be liked, but to be "well-liked." These hollow phrases demonstrate the inadequacy of language in conveying answers to Willy's search for meaning. In fact, at one point in the play, Willy asks Bernard outright, "What--what's the secret?" (*Salesman*, p. 92). If one exists, obviously it cannot be articulated. Rather than to reveal a truth, language is used in the play to maintain a false illusion. As Arthur Oberg notes, "The Lomans . . . use formulated wisdom to hold off the night when they will have to acknowledge what they evade, unhappiness and failure."[15] For Oberg, Miller's "stylized speech," like Pinter's, represents "the shrinkage and simplification of living made possible by cliche."[16]

In absurdist drama, language is inadequate as a method of conveying meaning. Esslin explains, "The Theatre of the Absurd . . . tends toward a radical devaluation of language, toward a poetry that is to emerge from the concrete and objectified images of the stage itself. . . . what *happens* on the stage transcends, and often contradicts, the *words* spoken by the characters" (*Absurd*, p. 26). With such a reduction in dialogue, the images presented to the audience become even more important. The same can be said of Miller's *Salesman*. As Orm Overland has written, "*Death of a Salesman* succeeds precisely because Willy's story is shown on stage, not told."[17] The images of reality, the scenes of past-in-present, the workings of the mind (as Miller's original conception of the set suggests) are more crucial to the production than the dialogue.

Cycle of the Play

Absurdist plays often end as they begin, forming a cycle. Because of this, Esslin explains, they seem to have "neither a beginning nor an end" (*Absurd*, p. 22). No ground has been gained, and no insight has been achieved by the characters. The audience is left with the sense that the action is perpetual.

In *Death of a Salesman*, Willy's kind of illusory thinking is perpetuated in his children. Incontestably, Willy dies in his illusion, and Hap continues in his father's illusion. However, many critics contend that Biff becomes aware of his identity and of his father's delusionary dream of success and chooses, by confronting his father, to abandon illusion. But an awareness of one's condition does not necessarily mean an abandoning of all illusion. Willy, facing the threat to his illusion of success as a salesman, transforms his illusion--to keep it alive--into an illusion of his son's success. Similarly, Biff may only trade his father's dream for one of his own. Joel Shatzsky explains: "Biff unequivocally presents his . . . own alternative to Willy's dream, but it is itself as tenuous as the salesman's: the 'agrarian myth.'"[18] Here Shatzsky refers to Biff's longing for a life outdoors, perhaps anticipating that ranching will fulfill his quest for personal identity, that he will "find himself" in that kind of work. According to absurdist philosophy, however, all illusions must be stripped away. In an absurd world lacking absolutes, the quest for meaning is equally absurd. Biff may be beginning to see that when he asks himself, after running out of Oliver's office, "Why am I trying to become what I don't want to be?" and when he tells his father, "Pop, I'm a dime a dozen and so are you!" (*Salesman*, p. 132). But at other times in the play, because he talks wistfully with Hap about a life out west, the audience cannot know for certain if Biff will ultimately leave all of his illusions behind. If he does not, says Shatzsky, the illusion he clings to would be "as much a myth as Willy's. . . ."[19]

There is another layer to the cycle of illusion, however; it involves the audience. If we can step back from the theatre and view the audience as part of the poetic image, watching the play, we can question whether they also perpetuate the illusion. As a type or symbol, Willy Loman provokes audience members to turn their thoughts inward. Though not absurdist, this form of identification with the character strengthens the absurdist cycle of the play by encouraging the audience to consider to what extent they continue to insist on meaning in their existences, to what extent they buy into the illusions of the myth Willy accepted. Most audiences, responding to *Salesman* as tragic, acknowledge the value system Willy accepts, and like Biff, recognize the illusion of that system, but, rather than abandoning the illusion, they identify with Willy and cling to it. The cycle is also perpetuated in each of them.

Perhaps the fact that this play has been widely hailed by audiences as a great modern tragedy demonstrates that they have accepted the illusion of the success myth. The success illusion is one embedded deep within society's structure; its values and "qualifications" for the individual, Miller tells us, have long been internalized.[20] Therefore, the play is more often considered the tragedy of *one man* rather than the absurdist destruction of an illusion.

As a result, *Death of a Salesman* has long been labeled a work of social realism. But a play need not carry a single label of style. As Esslin points out, "some of the elements of the Theatre of the Absurd can be combined with those of the conventional well-made play to produce a fruitful fusion of the two different traditions" (*Absurd*, p. 123). Absurdist playwrights Adamov, Ionesco, and Pinter have skillfully demonstrated in their works that a blend of absurdism and realism can be achieved. Certainly we should add Arthur Miller's name to the list, for in *Death of a Salesman* he has anticipated the absurdism of those later playwrights.

Notes

[1] Enoch Brater, "Miller's Realism and *Death of a Salesman*" in *Arthur Miller: New Perspectives*, ed. Robert A. Martin (Englewood Cliffs: Prentice-Hall, 1982), p. 115.

[2] See Robert F. Whitman, "The Nature and Kinds of 'Reality' in Drama" in *The Play-Reader's Handbook* (Indianapolis: Bobbs-Merrill, 1966), pp. 1-73; Esther Merle Jackson, "*Death of a Salesman*: Tragic Myth in the Modern Theater," *College Language Association Journal*, 7 (1963), 63-76; Arthur K. Oberg, "*Death of a Salesman* and Arthur Miller's Search for Style," *Criticism*, 9 (1967), 303-11; Murray Schumach, "Arthur Miller Grew in Brooklyn," *New York Times*, 6 February 1949, Sec. 2, p. 1+; and Joel Shatzky, "The 'Reactive Image' in Miller's *Death of a Salesman*," *Players*, 48 (1973), 104-10. Whitman and Jackson identify Miller's use of image in *Salesman* as departing from realistic tradition. Jackson also notes the play's aesthetic mode of development and subordination of language to image. Arthur Oberg examines Miller's devaluation of language further. And Murray Schumach and Joel Shatzky discuss the cycle of illusion perpetuated in the play.

[3] See, for example, Steven R. Centola, "Freedom and Responsibility After the Fall: A Sartrean Perspective of Arthur Miller's Existential Humanism," Diss. Univ. of Rhode Island 1981; Remy G. Saisselin, "Is Tragic Drama Possible in the Twentieth Century?" *Theatre Annual*, 17 (1960), 12-21; and Ronald Hayman, "Arthur Miller: Between Sartre and Society," *Encounter*, 37 (Nov. 1971), 73-79. Centola rejects the possibility of an absurdist staging of *Salesman*, claiming that Miller "do[es] not fit into the mainstream of absurdist dramatists who write about the absurd" (p. 48). Saisselin initially considers Miller in terms of the absurdist convention but then rejects the connection. For Saisselin, Willy "is not an absurd man; he is merely pathetic" (p. 20). Hayman also rejects the connection because he maintains that Miller attempts "to make meaningful statements about causal connections between one event and another," particularly between past and present events, and social and psychological events, and that the resulting pull "in different directions by social commitment on the one hand and formal experiment on the other" (p. 73) is damaging and troublesome in a single play.

[4] See C. J. Gianakaris, "Absurdism Altered: *Rosencrantz & Guildenstern Are Dead*," *Drama Survey*, 7 (Winter 1968-69), 52-58. Gianakaris responds to Miller's rejection of absurdism in his 1968 interview with Joan Barthel, "Arthur Miller Ponders *The*

Price," *New York Times*, 28 January 1968, Sec. 2, pp. 1, 5, in which Miller opposes its "devaluation of human existence."

[5] Arthur Miller, *Timebends: A Life* (New York: Grove, 1987), p. 314. All further references to this work will appear in the text.

[6] Martin Esslin, *Theatre of the Absurd*, 3rd ed. (New York: Penguin Books, 1980), p. 25. All further references to this work will appear in the text.

[7] Sandra Page Turney, "An Examination of Martin Esslin's Concept of the Absurdist Theatre as an Expression of Camus's Concept of Absurdity Set Forth in 'The Myth of Sisyphus,'" M.A. Thesis North Texas State Univ. 1976, p. 40.

[8] Letter received from Arthur Miller, 12 September 1991.

[9] Arthur Miller, "Introduction to the *Collected Plays*" in *The Theater Essays of Arthur Miller*, ed. Robert A. Martin (New York: Penguin, 1978), pp. 113-70.

[10] Brater, p. 120.

[11] Arthur Miller, *Death of a Salesman* (New York: Viking, 1949), p. 11. All further references to this work will appear in the text.

[12] Whitman, p. 48.

[13] Martin Erwin, "The Use of Blocks of Past Time in Arthur Miller's *Death of a Salesman*," M.A. Thesis University of North Carolina 1964, p. 3.

[14] Jackson, p. 70.

[15] Oberg, p. 308.

[16] Oberg, p. 309.

[17] Orm Overland, "The Action and Its Significance: Arthur Miller's Struggle with Dramatic Form," *Arthur Miller: New Perspectives*, p. 39.

[18] Shatzsky, p. 109.

[19] Shatzsky, p. 109.

[20] Arthur Miller, "The *Salesman* Has a Birthday" in *The Theater Essays of Arthur Miller*, p. 15.

John Proctor:
Christian Revolutionary

Timothy Miller

" . . . on Earth
Who Against Faith and Conscience can be heard
Infallible? yet many will presume. . . ."
Paradise Lost 12.529-31

In Arthur Miller's *The Crucible*, John Proctor separates himself from other Christians at Salem by avoiding public worship and refusing to have his youngest child baptized. Despite the warnings of Reverends Parris and Hale, he apparently thinks that he and his family can live and be saved without the services of the Salem church. Since church and state matters were tied together in the seventeenth century, his critical attitude toward the church brings him into conflict with civil as well as religious authorities.[1] Although his enemies see him as dangerous, he tries to do what is right in spiritual and civil affairs, hoping to change the Salem church as well as the court but finally rejecting both. He justifies his actions by the spiritual principles that grow out of his attitude toward the church--namely, that group or institutional authority cannot interfere with his conscience. Like others in the seventeenth century, he believes that his religious faith gives him direct knowledge of ultimate truth which institutions cannot contradict.[2] Therefore he remains suspicious of Salem's church and court and does not hesitate to rebel when his conscience differs from theirs.

Miller's historical commentary shows how deeply the Salem church was affected by social, political, and financial interests. Reverend Parris, who typifies the influence of the material upon the spiritual, hardly ever acts unless to protect his position as minister or to secure material items, like the deed to his house or the "golden candlesticks." In addition, he fears the power that church members have to order their own affairs: to appoint or depose their minister, to excommunicate members (as they do Proctor after he is convicted of witchcraft), and to override his request that an outsider like Reverend Hale come to Salem. Parris also preaches too much about Hell and too little about God, and he threatens those who lose loyalty to him with retaliation: "There is either obedience," he says, "or the church will burn like Hell is burning."[3]

Faced with a materialistic, authoritarian, and vindictive minister, believers turn away from the church, but Proctor himself never feels deprived of any spiritual benefits that come to believers who attend church. While his affair with Abigail changes almost everything else, it does not change his spiritual independence which is sustained some other way.

Proctor refuses to be bound by the local or the "central church" (*The Crucible*, p. 97). He tells Reverend Hale, for example, that he sees "no light of God" in Reverend Parris even though he is "ordained" (*The Crucible*, p. 65). Evidently, Proctor has experienced this light; he knows that it identifies a minister, but that Reverend Parris does not have it and is therefore unfit. The extent of his challenge measures his faith in the light. He defies not only two ordained ministers on spiritual matters, but also the spiritual hierarchy that ordained them, presumably the "central church." Proctor also confronts Parris, a Harvard educated minister, about what is good to hear in church, contending that he has the right to speak his heart (*The Crucible*, p. 30). Parris in turn rightly calls him a Quaker because, in the Quaker tradition, his conscience forces him to question ministerial control over preaching.[4] Since Proctor has no fear of overstepping his authority as a believer, he must think that his religion is between him and God alone.

Indeed, the church has little if any role in Proctor's life. While he agrees when Reverend Hale tells him that his house is not a church, he still has made it into one by praying there on Sundays instead of in the Salem church. Although he helped to build it, he does not need the church to pray, nor does he need the fellowship of public devotion. His action contradicts Hale who says that on the Sabbath a Christian must be in church (*The Crucible*, p. 65). Most Protestants, however, could not conceive of their spiritual life without a church, its "word and ordinances" (*The Crucible*, p. 4) being the normal channels by which God's grace reached believers. They thought that this was how God wanted to be worshiped.[5] Nevertheless, Proctor feels free to work out his own form of worship, believing that his private devotion is truer than church services and that God's grace comes to him directly.

Quakerism aptly describes the kind of threat that Proctor poses. The Quakers emphasized the inner religious experience of believers over the formal or institutional elements of Christianity which they regarded with contempt. Since God Himself communicated the Inward Light, the main doctrine of the Quakers, there was no need for a church and clergy to interpret it.[6] If all this applies to Proctor, it would imply that his anticlericalism may go beyond the contempt he feels for Reverend Parris. It would imply that he also opposes Parris because he does not think that as a minister he has any real function. In fact, Proctor's seeing no "light of God" in Parris or his speaking his "heart" to challenge him threatens the church just as the Quakers did--for the divine light in the conscience shows institutions to be a hindrance. It cannot be overruled by earthly authority.[7]

Though probably not a full-fledged Quaker, Proctor exiles himself from the Salem church in a way that suggests the mood of Quakerism. He remains true to his perception that his conscience sufficiently directs him independent of the church. In the seventeenth century, his rationale is a necessary outlook for a rebel spirit. Nevertheless, he is not excommunicated prior to his being convicted of witchcraft, and then only a portion of the church's members show up to vote against him (The Crucible, p. 128). Although he has rejected the present church, taking considerable latitude in religious practice, church members do not hold that against him. They recognize that he does not "desire the destruction of religion" (The Crucible, p. 66) and may sympathize with his religious individualism.

If Proctor's view of the church is in accord with anybody else's, it is that of the respected landowner Francis Nurse who says that his "wife is the very brick and mortar of the church" (The Crucible, p. 71); that is, believers are the living members of the church which Christ heads (1 Cor. 12.12-27, Eph. 4.11-16, Col. 1.18). The Nurse family has, in fact, already been involved in a separation from the Salem church (The Crucible, p. 26). Therefore, Reverend Parris and landowner Putnam, while enemies, have reason to fear that others will be influenced by Proctor's ideas and that they might follow him in rebelling against the church. In addition, because of Proctor's attitude toward the church, Reverend Hale tests his Christianity, and Parris doubts it in order to discredit his challenge to the court. Of course, after the introduction of witchcraft into the Salem community and after Mary Warren charges him as the "Devil's man," Proctor's spiritual life appears even more suspect and strange.

When his adultery comes back upon him in a new way through Abigail's charges, Proctor decides that his personal life will have the same honesty that his spiritual life has: "Now Hell and Heaven grapple on our backs, and all our old pretense is ripped away. . . . It is a providence, and no great change; we are only what we always were, but naked now" (The Crucible, pp. 80-81). Like other Puritans, Proctor sees his life in terms of the cosmic struggle between God and Satan for the fate of humanity.[8] Though Abigail has revealed their affair, he takes up his part in the struggle, going to the court to defend Elizabeth and others accused. He makes a fresh beginning: he tries to follow his conscience in relation to others the way he does in relation to God. It is his most difficult task.

Proctor probably did not expect corruption at court anymore than he did at church. The court, however, subverts normal due process by making the accuser "holy." Reverend Hale and Judge Danforth justify extraordinary legal and spiritual actions by claiming that they live in "new times" (*The Crucible*, pp. 71, 94). Some Puritans did, in fact, believe themselves to be living in a "new age," one in which they might justly expect "new light" or additional Inward Light from the Holy Spirit.[9] In Salem, however, the "new" revelation that "the voice of Heaven is speaking through the children" (*The Crucible*, p. 88) fulfills the expectation. For this reason as well as its own self-interest, the court inverts the moral order, "pulling Heaven down and raising up a whore" (*The Crucible*, p. 120). If there is no moral right, "God is dead," as Proctor says. Moreover, Mary Warren, his witness against Abigail, accuses him of witchcraft. The insecurity and guilt he feels about his personal life complicates the circumstances.

Despite all that, on the authority of his conscience, Proctor challenges the court's "contention" that "the voice of Heaven" speaks through the children. He questions not only its ability to determine legal guilt and innocence, but also its ability to identify, interpret, and carry out divine revelation. Once again, he opposes an institution that claims interpretative authority or control over God's will. This time he faces imprisonment and death from the court as well as excommunication from the church, yet he must try to maintain moral honesty and sincerity.

After making amends with Elizabeth, Proctor suggests to her that he might lie to win his life, but she tells him that only he can decide: "There is no higher judge under Heaven than Proctor is" (*The Crucible*, p. 130). When Parris, Danforth, and Hale urge him to lie to protect themselves, Proctor knows that he can look nowhere but to himself and God--it "is no part of salvation" (*The Crucible*, p. 143) that they use him. Since Reverend Hale cannot "read" God's will for him--indeed, no one can--Proctor himself, not the church, has the keys of heaven (Matt.16.19). He therefore keeps his moral choice free of the court as well as of the church: "And there's your first marvel, that I can. . ." (*The Crucible*, p. 144). He contrasts his actions with those of others: the divine grace and insight that had comforted and directed him in the past shows him how to be true to himself, to others unjustly condemned, and to God. As Hale's objections show, something astonishing, beyond reason and logic, tells him that it is right to die to keep the truth. The court may see the "marvel," but cannot recognize it when it occurs.

Three times in the play Proctor tells Mary Warren, "Do that which is good, and no harm shall come to thee," quoting from the apocryphal Book of Tobit (12.7). The text sums up his position. Like the angel Raphael, Proctor encourages a younger figure like the boy Tobias to acknowledge the truth in public and to believe that God will keep watch over him.[10] Unlike Mary Warren, however, Proctor does "that which is good," acknowledging the truth and trusting that God will not abandon him. Consequently, he finds some "shred of goodness" (*The Crucible*, p. 144) in himself; to find any more than that would be presumption to most Christians. Despite the judgment at Salem and the church's excommunication, Proctor knows that "no harm" will come to him--that God will admit him into heaven. As the saintly but condemned Rebecca Nurse says, "Another judgment awaits us all."[11] Proctor's apocryphal text, rejected by the historical church as unauthentic, justifies the only authentic course of action open to him: defiance of the court and church in confidence of God.

Proctor's life and death, like his apocryphal text, shows that his relationship with God remains outside the normal institutional channels. He earns his salvation independently, through faithful actions which often do not appear to be right in the eyes of others. Elizabeth correctly refuses to judge Proctor: God will judge him according to the light he has received (*The Crucible*, p. 130). In a way Judge Danforth never intended (*The Crucible*, p. 139), Proctor exemplifies the supreme moral courage of one who says no to the whole world because of his conscience. Nevertheless, he does not win his "shred of goodness" by withdrawing from the society of others, both alive and dead, as Hale would have him do through confession. Instead, he carries the strengths of his spiritual life with him into the court, standing up for right in an unjust world; his death hastens the "overthrow" of the Salem court and Parris' departure from the Salem church. His rebellion inspires a revolution.

As the epigraph to this paper suggests, Milton would have sympathized with Miller's portrait of nobility--of conscience over convenience. If the archangel Michael had asked that question

> on Earth
> Who Against Faith and Conscience can be heard
> Infallible?

John Proctor as well as John Milton would have said: nobody. They both were Christian revolutionaries, advocates of faith and conscience, adversaries of institutions.[12]

Notes

[1] I believe that Miller's treatment of Puritanism focuses more on questions pertaining to the individual's relation to religious and civil authorities and institutions than it does on questions of theology or doctrine. For a discussion of *The Crucible* in terms of Puritan "Covenant" theology, see Stephen Fender, "Precision and Pseudo

Precision in *The Crucible*," *Journal of American Studies*, 1 (1967), 87-98; and E. Miller Budick, "History and Other Spectres in Arthur Miller's *The Crucible*," *Modern Drama*, 28 (1985), 535-52. For a discussion of the play in terms of its immediate sources, see Robert A. Martin, "Arthur Miller's *The Crucible*: Background and Sources," *Modern Drama*, 20 (1977), 279-92.

[2] Miller's John Proctor appears to share in the radical reaction against all forms of Christian churches which occurred in the seventeenth century. It led to the view that traditional churches themselves were not essential to Christian devotion and to the view that the Holy Spirit was the supreme guide to faith and practice. Quakerism was one manifestation of this historical development; see Hugh Barbour, *The Quakers in Puritan New England* (New Haven: Yale University Press, 1964); and Geoffrey F. Nuttall, *The Holy Spirit in Puritan Faith and Experience* (Oxford: Blackwell, 1946).

Also see Rufus M. Jones, *The Quakers in the American Colonies* (1911; rpt. New York: Russell and Russell, 1962). Jones quotes from a letter written by a Quaker missionary in 1657 which indicated that Salem, Massachusetts, was a rich field, and he notes that radical influences had been at work there for some time. One of these influences was Roger Williams (1603?-1683), the "independent" lay preacher who favored complete separation of church and state; he had been chosen as minister of the Salem congregation in 1631 and again in 1634 (pp. 64-65). Williams, of course, went on to secure his charter for Rhode Island, the colony founded on the principles of church-state separation and religious toleration. His presence at Salem must have left its mark.

[3] Arthur Miller, *The Crucible* (Harmondsworth: Penguin, 1976), p. 30. All further references to this work will appear in the text.

[4] For example, see George Fox, *The Journal of George Fox*, ed. John L. Nickalls, rev. ed. (London: Religious Society of Friends, 1975). Fox consistently challenged ministers as interpreters of God's Word (pp. 24, 39-40, 76, and 93-94). His contempt for the clergy and his contempt for their churches ("steeplehouses") were well known. The doctrine of the universal Inward Light led him, like other Quakers, to the view that the clergy had no authority over scripture that other Christians did not have. In fact, the same Holy Spirit that inspired the Apostles inspired believers. See Fox, pp. 29-35; and Robert Barclay, *Barclay's Apology in Modern English*, ed. Dean Freiday (Elberon: n.p., 1967).

Robert Barclay (1648-1690), a second generation Quaker, issued *An Apology for the True Christian Divinity* first in Latin (1676) and then in English (1678) to explain Quaker belief systematically. The Quakers, however, attached no special importance to it. I cite from the modernized and abridged form of Barclay's *Apology* which is readily available.

[5] Most Protestants thought that the New Testament required certain forms of worship to be used in the church, mainly preaching of the Word and administration of the sacraments. These two main ordinances constituted the "marks" or attributes of the church. See, for example, John Calvin, *Institutes of the Christian Religion*, trans. Ford Lewis Battles, ed. John T. McNeill (Philadelphia: Westminster, 1960), p. 2.1024.

[6] See, for example, Fox, pp. 29-33, 103; and Barclay, pp. 112-13, 209-11.

[7] See, for example, Fox, p. 109.

[8] For an account of this struggle as described in Puritan sermons, see William Haller, *The Rise of Puritanism* (1938; rpt. Philadelphia: University of Pennsylvania Press, 1972), pp. 142-43, 152-61. *Paradise Lost* shows Milton's description of the great drama of salvation so dear to Puritans (12.358-360).

[9] For an account of the new historic sense that some Puritans felt, see Nuttall, pp. 102-04.

[10] Proctor repeats the words of the angel Raphael who explains to the boy Tobias that God's works must be acknowledged publicly and that God watches over those who trust in him (12.7). Tobias had much to acknowledge: he had survived a dangerous journey to get to his intended bride Sarah, who had been given in marriage to seven husbands, but an evil spirit named Asmodeus killed all of them on the wedding night. Tobias, however, survived his wedding night by following Raphael's advice to burn the heart and liver of a fish, the smell of which caused Asmodeus to flee to "Upper Egypt" where Raphael bound him (8.3). Tobias also found a cure for his father's blindness and returned with Sarah to Nineveh where his father lived, although he eventually went back to Media, his wife's home. The Book of Tobit clearly shows God's providential concern for His people. It seems to have caught the attention of seventeenth-century artists. For example, it provided Milton with material (*Paradise Lost* 4.166-71, 5.219-23, not to mention the fact that he has the angel Raphael instruct Adam and Eve) and Rembrandt (*The Angel departing from Tobit and his family*).

[11] See Arthur Miller, "Introduction to the *Collected Plays*" in *The Theater Essays of Arthur Miller*, ed. Robert A. Martin (New York: Penguin, 1978), p. 160. Here Miller writes: ". . . it is no mean irony that the theocratic prosecution should seek out the most religious people for its victims. . . ."

[12] Milton shares in the radical reaction against the institutional church that Miller's John Proctor shares in (see Note 2); for Milton's views toward the church in *Paradise Lost*, see Timothy Miller, "Milton's Religion of the Spirit and 'the state of the Church' in Book XII of *Paradise Lost*," *Restoration: Studies in English Literary Culture, 1660-1700*, 13 (1989), 7-16.

The Tragedy of Ethical Bewilderment

Qun Wang

Arthur Miller's plays thrive on their aesthetic as well as their ethical appeal. The playwright's antithetical approach is usually built on a contraposition to not only accentuate the equivocal nature of Miller's characters' perception and commitment but also, when solution fades into eventuality, divulge their potential for tragedy. In analyzing the cause for Willy Loman's emotional suffering, Miller posits that Willy

> was the kind of man you see muttering to himself on a subway, decently dressed, on his way home or to the office, perfectly integrated with his surroundings excepting that unlike other people he can no longer restrain the power of his experience from disrupting the superficial sociality of his behavior. Consequently he is working on two logics which often collide.[1]

On the surface level, the statement underlines the power of experience and questions its sometimes pernicious impact on a person who has lost the ability to disentangle himself from his past. But on a deeper level, Miller's postulation also reveals his belief that when a person, entrapped in the conflict between the two logics, "does not have a grip on the forces of life and has no sense of values which will lead him to that kind of grip,"[2] moral confusion and ideological bewilderment can very easily mislead him into committing himself to values that betray the character's true interests in life. It is arguable whether "the forces of life" in Miller's lexicon are identifiable with the power of the moral truth the dramatist has consistently been objectifying in his plays. What is clear is that it is in moral confusion that Miller sees one of the inexhaustible sources for tragedy in modern life.

In Bhaskara Panikkar's book, *Individual Morality and Social Happiness in Arthur Miller*, the author oversimplifies Miller's dexterous treatment of the dilemma of modern existence by arguing that Joe Keller, Willy Loman, and

Walter Franz are consenting victims violating the moral code and obeying the dictates of society. They lack self-will, self-knowledge, and self-awareness and therefore they are immoral."[3] He goes on to conclude that Joe Keller is really no better than a criminal, Willy Loman a deceiver, and Walter Franz an imposter. Not only is Panikkar's judgment of these characters misleadingly negative, but his assumption also denies any possible tragic implication in the sufferings of Miller's characters.

It is true that in their pursuit of business success, Miller's characters sometimes overlook their social responsibility; other times they exhibit an awkward inadequacy in dealing with their individual reality because of the lack of self-knowledge; and they invariably have to take moral responsibility for their commitment. But their mistakes result largely from their ideological confusion rather than from their moral conviction and their sense of guilt is what distinguishes them from irredeemable villains.

In *All My Sons*, *Death of a Salesman* and *The Price*, Miller's main characters all experience some kind of moral struggle. In *All My Sons*, Miller presents a character who only knows how to define his identity in terms of his social success and embraces public recognition as the only judgment of the validity of his actions. The audience, nevertheless, confronts two Kellers in the play: on one hand, Keller's humanity is firm in his loyalty to his family, in his love for kids, and in his attempt to redeem himself after the perpetration of an act of public betrayal; but, on the other hand, he appears to be too myopic to recognize the ethical implication of his actions and too pragmatic to resist all the glamorous temptations of commercial success. Keller's betrayal of the public trust thus is paralleled by and correspondent to the betrayal of his true self and of his true interests in life. A person who lacks moral conviction is doomed to be tormented by having to live beset by contradictions.

Throughout the play, we can feel Keller's sometimes painful groping for an answer to the conflict between his sense of achievement and his sense of guilt. However, because he is unable to see the moral equivocality of the social environment, Keller is fated to live in confusion when he evaluates his actions in terms of social acceptance and recognition:

> The story was, I pulled a fast one getting myself exonerated. So I get out of my car, and I walk down the street. But very slow. And with a smile. The beast! I was the beast; the guy who sold cracked cylinder heads to the Army Air Force; the guy who made twenty-one P-40's crash in Australia. Kid, walkin' down the street that day I was guilty as hell. Except I wasn't, and there was a court paper in my pocket to prove I wasn't, and I walked . . . past . . . the porches. Result? Fourteen months later I had one of the best shops in the state again, a respected man again; bigger than ever.[4]

The hesitation and the reflective movement in Keller's speech suggest a groping struggle. His seeming conviction does not cover the fact that Keller, dimly aware of the severe consequence of what he did in the war, is still earnestly searching for a way to clarify his moral confusion.

When Keller plays the policeman game with kids, he becomes his own detective and judge of conscience, subconsciously accepting his sense of guilt for the act of public betrayal he committed during the war. There is indeed no real jail in Keller's house. Kate Keller, in fact, says to one of her husband's playmates: "Stop that, Bert. Go home. . . . There's no jail here" (*All My Sons*, p. 74). But there is a true prisoner of conscience, evident when Joe says: "Bert, on my word of honor, there's a jail in the basement" (*All My Sons*, p. 65). Keller's offer to take care of the Deever family is another indication of his desperate attempt to sooth his conscience by partially acknowledging his responsibility. Steve Deever's presence in *All My Sons*, thus, has a vicarious function. Not only does he physically go to prison for Keller; he is also used as a surrogate in Keller's attempt to justify his decision to send defective cylinders to the Army Air Force during the war.

Keller's confessional impulse and his eagerness to accept the circumstantial justification to defend his decision objectify Keller's inner struggle, or what Miller calls "the war within the self"[5]--while he vehemently attempts to convince himself of the validity of his action, he also dimly recognizes the devastating consequence and the negative moral implication of his action. When Joe Keller decides to take his own life, the action consummates a long trip in search of reconciliation between his senses of guilt and accomplishment. It is more than an attempt to clear the trail for the future of his family. It is also his way of accepting his responsibility in a self-imposed trial, judgment, and sentence. In *All My Sons*, Keller is as much tortured by his sense of guilt as he is victimized by his illusions about the importance of business success--illusions that blind him to his moral responsibility.

In a land seen by many as a place full of infinite opportunities Willy Loman, confused about his true identity and disheartened by his failure in pursuit of business success, cries fire. When an opportunistic proclivity threatens to obliterate the last of the already dimly recognizable traces of individual probity, Arthur Miller challenges the values of commerce by impugning their ethical justifiability. In *Death of a Salesman*, Miller again raises a moral question. Willy Loman's apparent psychological derangement is marked as much by hallucinations about his past as by confusion about the present. If *All My Sons* is a study of a character whose lack of moral conviction precipitates the moral crisis, *Death of a Salesman* is about how a character is destroyed both mentally and physically by his commitment to false values, values which misrepresent the character's true interests in life.

In *Death of a Salesman*, Willy Loman's problem is not so much that he cannot effectively separate himself from his past as that "He never knew who he was."[6] Loman's problem dealing with his past experience is not what misleads him into accepting his defeat in business as the end of life. What blinds him to the distinction between defeat in business and defeat in life is his belief that he cannot live by any identity other than that designated to him by society. This belief blocks his view from any other alternatives in life.

Throughout *Death of a Salesman*, "the war within the self" reveals to the audience Willy Loman's dichotomous side. The play's tragic effect hangs very heavily on the intensity of the conflict between two Willy Lomans: Willy the innocent and Willy the imposter. The conflict is suggested in Willy's opening speech when he complains about the invasion of the "strange thoughts" (*Salesman*, p. 132). The word "strange" apparently accentuates a sense of alienation. But what appears to be Willy's lament over his bout with hallucinations of his past experience, on the symbolic level of the play, summarizes his whole life: Willy Loman becomes a moral invalid when he accepts the dream of business success as the ultimate goal in life and the values of commerce as the guide of his actions. When Willy Loman is mesmerized by "thoughts" that do not reflect his true interests in life, he becomes a stranger to himself.

In *Death of a Salesman*, Willy's moral confusion is suggested by a struggle between the two Willys, often confronting and challenging each other in the open. Part him consecrates the law of the jungle as the only tutelage under which one can achieve financial success and social prominence. He teaches his sons the kinds of values which defy any ethical restrictions; he exposes his egocentricity in being overly concerned with his likableness; and he betrays Linda's trust with his infidelity. But there is another part of Willy which questions the moral justifiability of the values he follows and tries to instill into his sons: "sometimes I'm afraid that I'm not teaching them the right kind of--Ben, how should I teach them?" (*Salesman*, p. 159).

The public Willy knows the rules of social games and warns his children about the importance of appearance and speech: "And don't say 'Gee.' 'Gee' is a boy's word. A man walking in for fifteen thousand dollars does not say 'Gee!'" (*Salesman*, p. 169). But the Willy in private enjoys using a childish language: "Gee, look at the moon moving between the buildings!" (*Salesman*, p. 172). Willy Loman's sometimes childish mentality, as reflected in his language and behavior--clearly criticized, for example, when Charley asks him, "When the hell are you going to grow up?" (*Salesman*, p. 192), shows the audience his innocent side which remains unaffected by social hypocrisy. Irrevocably stuck in the conflict between his two selves, Loman is, paradoxically, as innocent as he is unscrupulous.

Finally, Willy the salesman makes a living with his appearance and mouth. But the true Willy Loman, on the contrary, wants to work with his hands. He proudly declares: "A man who can't handle tools is not a man" (*Salesman*, p. 154), while apparently being ignorant of the disparity between what he wants to accomplish in life and what he is supposed to. Linda's comment at the requiem further accentuates this discrepancy in Willy's life: "He was so wonderful with his hands" (*Salesman*, p. 221). Indeed, we can always sense in the play that there is another side of Willy Loman which is tired of playing the game of social pretension and eager to take control of his own destiny.

The Price is considered by many critics a continuation of the saga of the Loman family. But, more importantly, the play also demonstrates a consistency in Miller's use of an antithetical approach built on contraposition. In *The Price*, "the war within the self" is transformed into a public confrontation between two brothers. In the antithetical contraposition between Walter Franz and Victor Franz, we see the reflection of the inner struggle in Joe Keller and Willy Loman.

In *The Price*, Walter and Victor manifestly represent two conflicting value systems as well as two contrasting views on society. Walter is the epitome of business success and the values of commerce, while Victor is the incarnation of a traditional sense of morality and social responsibility. Victor, as his name indicates, appears to be morally superior, since he is the one who sacrifices his academic pursuit to fulfill his social responsibility, while Walter is a bona fide victim of the prevailing value system, who loses his objective in life in his pursuit of business success.

Instead of taking a good-guy and bad-guy approach, *The Price* examines the complexities of modern life by using a paradoxical juxtaposition. Apart from the apparent ideological and moral differences between the two characters, both brothers build their sense of achievement on their superficial understanding of reality. Walter, in pursuing the dream of wealth and social recognition, overlooks the fact that, in losing his individual integrity, he becomes "a kind of instrument, an instrument that cuts money out of people, or fame out of the world."[7] Victor is so firm in his commitment to his ideal he is also living in his "fantasy," moral conviction blinding him to reality. Both brothers live a frenzied life and both must pay for their illusive dreams: Walter with his past and Victor with his future. The incapacitating nature of both Walter and Victor's fantasy world is accentuated through the portrayal of both characters' emotional sufferings. The conflict between the characters' illusions and reality again constitutes the central contrariety of *The Price* and precipitates the development of its plot.

In Miller's theater, the use of an antithetical approach reveals the dichotomous side of his characters. These characters sometimes find it hard to disentangle themselves from the memory of the past; they sometimes are confused about their individual identities in pursuit of social recognition and acceptance; and they appear pathetic in committing themselves to morally dubious values. But their humanity is firmly established by their aspiration for human dignity, secured by their belief in change, accentuated by their longing for family harmony, and even suggested in their courage to cling obstinately to their commitment. They taunt us with their mishaps; they challenge our sense of security and complacency with their sufferings; and they even solicit our sympathies.

Miller defines truth in terms of his characters' moral soundness. Reality in Miller's theater, thus, is not so much employed to accentuate the relativity of truth as to challenge the validity of his characters' perception and commitment. Truth might be relative to human perceptions, but the tragic suffering of a character who is caught in the central conflict found in most of Miller's plays is too physically real and painful to suggest the acceptability of a solipsistic interpretation of reality.

Notes

[1] Arthur Miller, Introduction, *Arthur Miller's Collected Plays* (New York: Viking, 1957), I, p. 25.

[2] Henry Popkin, "Arthur Miller: The Strange Encounter," in *American Drama and Its Critics*, ed. John D. Hurrell (New York: Scribner's, 1961), p. 50.

[3] N. Bhaskara Panikkar, *Individual Morality and Social Happiness in Arthur Miller* (Atlantic Highlands: Humanities, 1982), p. 11.

[4] Arthur Miller, *All My Sons* in *Arthur Miller's Collected Plays* (New York: Viking, 1957), I, p. 80. All further references to this work will appear in the text.

[5] Arthur Miller in Interview with Henry Brandon, "The State of the Theater, a Conversation with Arthur Miller," *Harper's*, Nov. 1960, p. 68.

[6] Arthur Miller, *Death of a Salesman* in *Arthur Miller's Collected Plays* (New York: Viking, 1957), I, p. 221. All further references to this work will appear in the text. appear in the text.

[7] Arthur Miller, *The Price* in in *Arthur Miller's Collected Plays* (New York: Viking, 1981), II, p. 350. All further references to this work will appear in the text. appear in the text.

Meeting Dr. Mengele:
Naming, Self (Re)presentation and the Tragic Moment in Miller

Jeanne Johnsey

Immediately following her performance as Madame Butterfly with the woman's orchestra at Birkenau Concentration Camp, Fania Fenelon is complimented by the infamous Dr. Mengele, who tells her, "I have rarely felt so totally--moved."[1] When Kramer, the camp Commandant, agrees with Mengele, he addresses his remarks to Fania, calling her by her stage name. Fania shocks everyone present by interrupting the Commandant to inform him that her real name is "Goldstein." She does this knowing that it calls attention to her position as a prisoner marked for death. "Fenelon was my mother's name," she tells the Commandant and Mengele; "My father's name was Goldstein. I am Fania Goldstein" (*Playing for Time*, p. 481). At this moment, Fania demonstrates the kind of tragic awareness Albert Camus describes in his essay on the myth of Sisyphus. It is the moment of pause before descending the mountain.

Similar moments, in which characters emphatically cry out their names, occur in other Miller plays such as *The Crucible* and *Death of a Salesman*. And these moments illuminate the entire body of Miller's drama. Gerald Weales has pointed out the value of "looking at [Miller's] work . . . through his heroes and . . . the concern of each . . . with his identity--his name."[2] In the particular episodes I will discuss, the characters insist on identifying with their names, in ways that delineate each individual's response to overwhelming external power.

In *The Crucible*, John Proctor goes to his death rather than sign his name to a false confession that would buy him his life. He tells Danforth, ". . . You will not use me! I am John Proctor!"[3] Later he cries, "I have given you my soul; leave me my name!" (*The Crucible*, p. 328). Willy Loman in *Death of a Salesman* refuses to accept the devaluation threatened by the marketplace when he cries to Biff, "I am not a dime a dozen! I am Willy Loman and you are Biff Loman!"[4] All of these characters are making points about their names that equate power with control of the name. Each character's response to this equation is an act of self-empowerment--however momentary it may seem in terms of external, objective reality. All of these acts are transformative for the characters in terms of self-realization.

In his autobiography, Miller recalls a moment of terror in a New York public library when he was asked to give his father's name. Although the six-year-old boy had never heard an anti-Semitic remark, he remembers that "a certain childish recognition of infinite human brutality" caused him to feel challenged by the librarian to "identify [him]self as a candidate for victimization." Unable to give the librarian his father's "so Jewish name, Isidore," he ran away.[5] The moments of self-empowerment for Fania, Proctor, and Willy might be read as Miller's attempt to recapture and rewrite the moment in his own past, to reinscribe that particular memory as a self-affirmation; in other words, in his plays, Miller can be said to explore what might have been.

Miller's desire to explore alternatives to the past is clear in *Death of a Salesman*. Throughout the play Willy's past is a palpable presence through which he continually replays his lost opportunity to follow his successful brother, Ben. "There's just one opportunity I had with that man," he tells Charley, and he continually revisits that one opportunity in memory.

Miller's proclivity for reclaiming past moments and exploring the "what ifs" of recollection is not limited to his own experience, as he shows in his discussion about writing *After the Fall* in response to Camus's novel *The Fall*. Miller explains:

> The springboard of the book is the failure of the hero--or anti-hero--to go to the rescue of a girl . . . . I changed the question posed in *The Fall*, probably to a more disastrous one: what if he had attempted to rescue her, and indeed managed to, and then discovered . . . that there were innumerable complications about rescuing somebody as a pure act of love?[6]

The question then becomes one of responsibility for choices. The individual's responsibility for the moment of decision continues to occupy Miller. At the same time, he remains sensitive to the personal impact of an individual's confrontation with power.

In one of his earliest memories, Miller recalls the dichotomy of individual versus power as he tells about sitting in his great-grandfather's lap in synagogue. He remembers having his questions silenced by the grown-ups, "lest God turn an impatient eye my way." Recalling that moment he says, "[T]he transaction called believing comes down to the confrontation with overwhelming power and then the relief of knowing that one has been spared its worst" (*Timebends*, p. 37).

Miller addresses humanly created power with a similar sense of awe when he shows an Eastern government, perhaps, spying on a group of writers in *The Archbishop's Ceiling*. In the introduction to that play, Miller asks what is done to one's very identity when "power's ear is most probably overhead?"[7]

Fania, Proctor, and Willy each stand face to face with a power that threatens their very identity with extinction, and they resist that power by invoking the power of their own names. As Neil Carson has pointed out, "There is a recurring refusal on the part of Miller's characters to accept without question the outside world's assessment of their character."[8] Willy Loman speaks directly to this issue when he cries, "I am not a dime a dozen!" (*Salesman*, p. 217).

For each of these characters, the self-nominative moment becomes that moment of consciousness which Camus describes with his Sisyphus analogy. According to the myth, Camus reminds us, Sisyphus is condemned to ceaselessly roll a rock to the top of a mountain. The rock always rolls down, and Sisyphus has to then roll it back up to the top of the mountain. Camus says:

> It is during that return, that pause, that Sisyphus interests me. . . . That hour like a breathing-space which returns as surely as his suffering, that is the hour of consciousness. At each of those moments when he leaves the heights and gradually sinks toward the lairs of the gods, he is superior to his fate. He is stronger than his rock. . . . If this myth is tragic, that is because its hero is conscious.[9]

Miller seems to address the same breathing space when he says in a television interview, "Most human enterprises disappoint. But between starting something and that ultimate disappointment we accomplish a great deal."[10]

The events of self-nomination in the cases of Miller's characters accomplish a great deal by providing significant interruption of culturally imposed realities. By invoking the power of their individual names, they each subvert the collective assumptions of prevailing power's institutions: the validity of the Nazi machine, the witch hunt and insistence on public confession, and the marketplace values are all called into question.

And these actions exemplify what Miller has defined as his idea of poetic theater. Miller describes his idea this way:

> What I wanted was a poetic theater . . . meaning that in one symbolic act you brought the society [and] individual psychology [in] conflict together, and it was all a fusion. . . . You looked to . . . the Greeks who managed in the shape of one or two conflicting characters a whole world in motion: a moral, physical, political, psychological world all at the same instant in a human being. That unification of all these forces in one is poetry. That's what I mean by poetry.[11]

When Fania states her name, she calls these forces into motion. She not only interrupts the Commandant's speech, but she also ruptures the narrative structure of the sham scenario that the camp officials have created. She reveals as fiction the idea that the concerts they attend bear any similarity to ordinary civilized cultural events, during which the normal relationships of artist and audience can be properly maintained.

Fania's declaration of her name at that particular moment exposes the absurdity of Mengele's genteel pose by calling attention to the fact that Fania, the performer whom he claims has moved him, stands before him in the camp because she has a name that his power group has decreed undesirable; indeed, the camp itself exists because of Hitler's ideology which rests on the notion that some names may be decreed undesirable. The brutal appropriation of power is placed in the spotlight. The seams of that particular reality are exposed. The political, moral, physical, and psychological forces involved in the upheaval of war, the brutality of the Nazi regime, the weight of massive human suffering, and the resistance to total surrender of human dignity come together in the conflict occurring in that camp, in that room, in that instant, in that one human psyche.

A similar unity of forces comes into play for John Proctor. The issue at stake for him is the sanctity of individual conscience against the state's power to invade and assert its undisputed version of truth about good and evil. Proctor demands, "Is there no good penitence but it be public? God does not need my name nailed upon the church! God sees my name; God knows how black my sins are! It is enough!" (*The Crucible*, p. 327). For Proctor, as for Fania, one's name becomes the last barricade, the last fall-back position. For Willy it is the only remaining bargaining chip, and it has to buy something dear.

What is at risk in *Death of a Salesman* is the worth of a human being measured against market values. Willy resists being marked-down. He will not wear the "dime a dozen" price tag. And the only words he can resist with are those that make up his name because even his own beliefs about who he is, and the way he connects with his world, must be formed in market-based words, which are the only words he has to express his every thought. He first criticizes Biff because he "has yet to make thirty-five dollars a week" (*Salesman*, p. 134) and then later praises him by saying, "I'll put my money on Biff" (*Salesman*, p. 135). He supports Biff's business plan by calling it "a one-million-dollar idea" (*Salesman*, p. 168). When he says to Biff "I am Willy Loman, and you are Biff Loman" (*Salesman*, p. 217), he attempts to pass on to Biff whatever value he can believe has accrued in that name. And when, ultimately, he goes to his death to leave Biff a legacy in the form of an insurance policy, Willy exalts, "Can you imagine that magnificence with twenty thousand dollars in his pocket?" (*Salesman*, p. 219).

The collision of public and private worlds in these pivotal moments brings the individual to crisis at the point Camus calls "the pause." Mark Taylor's comments on the connections between identity, time, and modality suggest a paradigm for locating identity in that pause:

> Identity includes two closely related elements: self-sameness at a particular time and continuity through time. . . . [T]ime is not made up of three separate tenses or three discrete moments. There is but one sense of time, the present. The present, moreover, is comprised of three inseparable modalities. Memory and expectation join in the present. . . . The activity of self-presentation constitutes a process of self-appropriation through which the subject comes into possession of itself. . . . [T]he subject realizes itself as self-present subjectivity. Only with this . . . does the subject assume its proper name. . . . The complex self-presence that results . . . mirrors the intricacy of the present itself. Self, as well as time, is *one* substance with *three* modes.[12]

In metaphysical terms, this view of the self can be understood, as Kierkegaard points out, in the following way: "The I-am-I is a mathematical point which does not exist. . . . It is only momentarily that the particular individual is able to realize existentially a unity of the infinite and the finite which transcends existence."[13] Miller's characters perform such acts of self-appropriation and transcendence.

The power of a name to achieve such pervasive effects is well established in modern critical theory. Innumerable aspects of the power dynamic are inherent in the act of naming. Naming is controlling, owning. Ralph Ellison has noted in his essay on the slave name phenomenon, "it is through our names that we first place ourselves in the world. Our names being gifts of others must be made our own."[14]

The moment of self-naming is the moment of choice, of proclaiming ownership and control of the self, of making our names our own. At the beginning of *Playing for Time*, Fania has given little thought to her Jewish identity. She resists joining in the factionalism among the other prisoners, she has no ideological agenda beyond her basic human one, and she refuses to say that Nazis are not human beings because that would dismiss the problem too easily. For her, the fact that they *are* human *is* the problem. As she tells a fellow prisoner, "we know a little something about the human race that we didn't know before. And it's not good news" (*Playing for Time*, p. 516). Fania chooses to define her connection with human reality by claiming her own space in that reality through taking possession and control of her name.

Proctor's choice is between real and false martyrdom. He makes his fake confession to save his life, but refuses to sign a written one because he recognizes that "What others say and what I sign to is not the same" (*The*

Crucible, p. 328). In his refusal to relinquish control over his name, Proctor becomes superior to his fate, as Sisyphus becomes stronger than his rock in the moment when he has pushed it to the heights and recognizes that it must fall back again. It is in this moment of realization that the protagonist defines himself/herself through his/her choices.

Willy, facing his dilemma, appears to waver toward external definition when he appeals to Howard for a job saying, "If I had forty dollars a week that's all I'd need" (*Salesman*, p. 181). But he ultimately chooses his subjective inner vision over the external view which for him means devaluation. Charlie seems to understand this when he tells Linda in the Requiem, "No man only needs a little salary" (*Salesman*, p. 221). Willy becomes this inner vision of himself when he cries, "I am Willy Loman!" and he becomes present in the act of representing himself.

In like manner, with the gesture of saying "I am Fania Goldstein," Fania performs the act of becoming Fania Goldstein and at that moment is present in the representation; the nominative act and the Self become one. She is presenting and at the same time re-presenting her Self. In that moment she achieves the unity of the infinite and finite and transcends existence momentarily, in the pause, in the moment of consciousness that Camus calls tragedy.

Notes

[1] Arthur Miller, *Playing for Time* in *Arthur Miller's Collected Plays* (New York: Viking, 1981), II, p. 481. All further references to this work will appear in the text.

[2] Gerald Weales, "Arthur Miller: Man and His Image," in *Death of a Salesman: Text and Criticism* (New York: Viking, 1967), p. 351.

[3] Arthur Miller, *The Crucible* in *Arthur Miller's Collected Plays* (New York: Viking, 1957), I, p. 327. All further references to this work will appear in the text.

[4] Arthur Miller, *Death of a Salesman* in *Arthur Miller's Collected Plays* (New York: Viking, 1957), I, p. 217. All further references to this work will appear in the text.

[5] Arthur Miller, *Timebends: A Life* (New York: Grove, 1987), p. 24. All further references to this work will appear in the text.

[6] Arthur Miller, as quoted in V. Rajakrishnan, "After Commitment: An Interview with Arthur Miller," in *Conversations with Arthur Miller*, ed. Matthew C. Roudané (Jackson: University Press of Mississippi, 1987), p. 336.

[7] Arthur Miller, "Introduction" in *The American Clock and The Archbishop's Ceiling: Two Plays* (New York: Grove, 1989), p. x.

[8] Neil Carson, *Arthur Miller* (New York: Grove, 1982), p. 97.

[9] Albert Camus, *The Myth of Sisyphus and Other Essays*. Trans. Justin O'Brien (New York: Knopf, 1969), p. 121.

[10] *Arthur Miller*, narr. Allan Yentab, prod. Kevin Loader, Arts and Entertainment Network, February 1989.

[11] *Arthur Miller*, Arts and Entertainment Network.

[12]Mark C. Taylor, *Erring: A Postmodern A/Theology* (Chicago: University of Chicago Press, 1987), pp. 37, 44.

[13]Soren Kierkegaard, *Concluding Unscientific Postscript to Philosophical Fragments.* Trans. and ed. Howard V. Hong and Edna M. Hong (Princeton: Princeton University Press, 1992), I, p. 197.

[14]Ralph Ellison, *Shadow and Act* (New York: Random House, 1964), p. 147

Arthur Miller and the Temptation of Innocence

Terry Otten

Given Arthur Miller's preoccupation with innocence and guilt, with the paradoxical nature of good and evil, with questions raised by the responsibility for choice and the often ambiguous consequences of moral actions, it is no wonder that lawyers, policemen, judges, and other representatives of the legal system haunt his plays or that court room scenes, literal or figurative, so often provide the settings for his dramas. In large measure Miller conceives of ignorance as the most morally destructive of all forces--ignorance disguised as innocence. Like Rollo May, he understands that though "it is dangerous to know, it is even more dangerous not to know,"[1] that it is not guilt that produces moral chaos but the specious claim of innocence, the most basic form of self-ignorance. Indeed, guilt, the very testimony of self-knowledge, alone can regenerate the redemptive power to restore moral equilibrium to a world he describes as "after the Fall."

I take as a starting point Leonard Moss's remark in regard to *After the Fall* that from the beginning of his career Miller had always had "a strong interest in the Fall theme," which Moss characterizes simply as "the crisis of disillusionment."[2] Although Moss does not examine the thesis in detail, even a cursory glance at Miller's plays reveals the Fall theme as a seminal motif in his work. Both explicit and implicit references allude to the myth, perhaps testifying to Miller's claim in the introduction to his *Collected Plays* that "Each of these plays, in varying degrees, was begun in the belief that it was unveiling a truth already known but unrecognized as such."[3]

Miller's perspective on the Fall often aligns with his view of the failure of the American dream. Repeatedly, he alludes to the dissociation between humanity and nature in American culture. The characterization of American society from *All My Sons* to *The American Clock* reveals a society already fallen, devoid of a spiritual center and the restorative powers of nature. Miller conceives of the American crisis in terms of the death of paradise, a lapsed culture destroyed by its materialism, an ironic, inverted image of an Eden lost from its very conception. As the old man Solomon tells Victor in *The Price*, "I mean it's already in the Bible, the rat race. The minute she laid her hand on the apple, that's it. . . . There's always a rat race, you can't stay out of it."[4]

In his first major play, *All My Sons* (1947), Miller evokes the idea of a collapsed Eden in the very setting, in the image of the fallen apple tree in the Kellers' back yard. As Joe, on the Sunday morning the play opens, sits reading the want ads, trying, he tells his neighbor Frank, "To see what people want," the newly fallen tree with *"fruit still clinging to its branches"*[5] signals the end of innocence. Planted to commemorate Larry's death, the tree symbolizes the composite lie which has to this point upheld the tenuous "Garden." Its destruction foretells the emerging revelation that the characters already live "after the fall," victims of a perverse quest for success and a vain attempt to conceal the guilt that all to some degree share.

Of course, *Death of a Salesman* contains numerous references to the alienation from nature and the idea of a shattered paradise. Willy's yearning for his past announced in the *"small and fine"* flute melody *"telling of grass and the horizon"*; his desire to be in New England where "the trees are so thick and the sun is warm"; his remembrance of the two elm trees, the lilac and wisteria, the peonies and daffodils; his illusion that he had opened the windshield on his car to feel the fresh air even though his car has no windshield; his goal to buy a farm and work with his hands; his illusory claim to Ben that "we hunt . . . snakes and rabbits--that's why I moved out here"--all his futile attempts to recover an innocent past stand in stark contrast to the reality that you "Gotta break your neck to see a star in this yard" and that "You can't see nothing out here! They boxed in the whole goddam neighborhood!"[6] Fully aware, as he twice says, that "The woods are burning" (*Salesman*, pp. 152, 199), he pleads with Ben, ". . . how do we get back to all the great times? Used to be so full of light, and comradeship, the sleigh-riding in winter, and ruddiness on his cheeks" (*Salesman*, p. 213), a desire mirrored in Biff's love of the range and his awareness that ". . . we don't belong in this nuthouse of a city! We should be mixing cement on some open plain, or--or carpenters" (*Salesman*, p. 166).

But the evocation of a past paradise proves meaningless in a society already doomed. Roslyn tells Gay in *The Misfits* that "It must have been wonderful" when they used to herd and ride the wild mustangs, but Gay knows too well that "They changed it. Changed it all around. They smeared it all over with blood, turned it into shit and money just like everything else. . . . It's like ropin' a dream now."[7] It is the same destructive force of materialism that reduces the walls of paradise to the confines of the car parts warehouse in *A Memory of Two Mondays*, which Bert describes as "a great big room" in which "We're riding back and forth . . . And no end ever! Just no end!"[8]

But it is not only ironic Edenic references that allude to Miller's adaptation of the Fall myth and portray the corruption of American values. More essentially, Miller employs the theme to confront the question of human responsibility. Perhaps no modern playwright has been so convinced of original sin, that is, of the human capacity and inclination to commit evil. He has commented that "I can't see the problem of will evolving fruitfully unless the existence of evil is taken into account."[9] The evasion of personal responsibility has been the common gesture of our age. Writes Miller, "[A]long came psychology to tell us that we were again the victims. . . . [W]e are equally irresponsible" (*Theater Essays*, p. 212). This twentieth-century version of reaching for fig leaves denies the essential benefit of the Fall--self-knowledge; for it is only by acknowledging personal culpability that human beings can be empowered "to make choices against evildoing," as Miller writes in his autobiography *Timebends*, "which is what helps to keep the good alive."[10]

Throughout his works, Miller's characters achieve a measure of heroism in so far as they accept their own guilt. As John Proctor tells Judge Danforth in *The Crucible*, "A fire, a fire is burning! I hear the boot of Lucifer, I see his filthy face! And it is my face, and yours, Danforth!"[11] Such complicity belongs even to those who do not commit apparent evil but engage in a conspiracy of accommodation by ignoring the truth and evading responsibility. When in *A View from the Bridge* Catherine cries out that Eddie belongs in the garbage can for turning in Rodolpho and Marco, Beatrice responds, "Then we all belong in the garbage. You, and me. . . . Whatever happened we all done it, and don't you ever forget it, Catherine."[12] Such communal guilt surfaces in *Incident at Vichy* as well when the Jewish doctor Leduc says to Prince Von Berg that there is in everyone's mind "a dislike if not hatred for the Jews" and that "Until you know it is in you you will destroy whatever truth can come of this atrocity."[13] Later he tells the Prince, "there is nothing and will be nothing--until you face your own complicity with this . . . your own humanity" (*Incident at Vichy*, p. 288). As he goes to his death, he comments, "I am only angry that I should have been born before the day when man has accepted his own nature, that he is *not* reasonable, that he is full of murder, that his ideals are only the little tax he pays for the right to hate and kill with a clear conscience" (*Incident at Vichy*, p. 287). Miller employs the "Jewish question" frequently to explore the nature of the composite guilt of humanity--not only in plays like *Incident at Vichy* and *After the Fall* but in his novel *Focus* and other works. In *Playing for Time*, his 1980 screenplay, when the actress Elzvieta asks Fania Fenelon to forgive her for judging her an acquiescent victim, Fania responds, "It's the other ones who are destroying us--and they only feel innocent."[14] And when Esther protests

Fania's calling their captors human, Fania asks, "Then what are they, Esther?" (*Playing for Time*, p. 516). Even the most sadistic are human, she tells Esther, "Like you. Like me" (*Playing for Time*, p. 484).

Conversely, those who claim innocence by consciously concealing their Cainlike nature can never escape the imprisonment of their debilitating Edenic state. They are like the anonymous government authorities in *The Archbishop's Ceiling* (1977) who keep repairing the 400-year-old angels on the ceiling, leading Sigmund to remark with obvious irony that "we shall have the most perfect angels in the whole world."[15]

Those who claim innocence prevent the redemptive, if potentially destructive, power of truth. This pattern of drama in which action moves climactically to the revelation of self-knowledge parallels what Miller sees as the rhythmic pattern of tragedy. He distinguishes between pathos, which can produce "sadness, sympathy, identification and even fear" and tragedy which, in addition, "brings us to knowledge or enlightenment" (*Theater Essays*, p. 9). The essential knowledge for Miller, what he calls the "secret thrust" of tragedy (*Timebends*, p. 519), self-awareness, marks the culmination of "the drive to make life real by conquering denial" (*Timebends*, p. 519). In short, the end of tragedy is the end of all claims of innocence and the tragic hero's acceptance of his own criminality. "And that's the victory," Miller says of Oedipus: "We need his crime. That crime is a civilizing crime" (*Theater Essays*, p. 269) in its capacity to affirm the moral order. We see something of the Romantic's version of the "fortunate fall": the attainment of self-knowledge that makes operative the regenerative force of tragedy by exposing the destructive potential in the self. The peace of Eden, Miller writes in the "Foreword" to *After the Fall*, existed only "because man had no consciousness of himself" and so no need for choice. When Eve "opened up the knowledge of good and evil, she presented Adam with a choice. So that where choice begins, Paradise ends, Innocence ends" (*Theater Essays*, p. 255). Eve created tragic paradox by assertion of will. The choice scarcely matters; either way she had to lose, either by disobeying the commandment or by denying her own will to know. Nor does it matter why God created the absurd dilemma. What does matter is that she chose and thereby gained the terrible truth that there is no reprieve from self-knowledge or the consequences of choice, that the evil that exists in the world is the creation of those who choose it, and that only the acceptance of responsibility for evil can abate its dominance.

Miller's conception of the Fall and its relationship to tragedy finds full expression in the two works that most directly allude to the myth, *After the Fall* and *The Creation of the World and Other Business*. Performed in 1972, eight years after *After the Fall*, *Creation* attempts to achieve what Miller himself called impossible in a 1960 discussion of Graham Greene's dramas:

the marrying of realism and religious or spiritual drama. Though Miller decried "the power of realism's hold in the theater" by the time he wrote *The Crucible* in 1953 (see Introduction to *Collected Plays* I, p. 46), his own best work has been grounded in realism, even when it pursues moral or ethical issues. Abandoning the elements of realism for fantasy and myth in *Creation*, Miller lapses into philosophical rhetoric and manipulation of characters as agents of discourse. Nonetheless, *Creation* examines the ancient questions of how a just God could allow "such monstrous acts" as Abel's murder and why He "has apparently designed mankind so as to perpetuate them" (*Timebends*, p. 558). Though at times obscure, the play confronts the paradox that surfaces often in Miller's plays: though no moral victory can be gained without escaping the tyranny of innocence, such self-awareness can produce paralyzing self-judgment.

Miller's characterization of God in *Creation* is rather ambiguous if not, in Kroll's term, "muddleheaded."[16] Lucifer psychoanalyzes the Deity, arguing that God put the Tree of Good and Evil in the garden "to tempt *Himself*," and that "He's not of one mind about innocence."[17] He assumes the role of God's own agent: "I disobey what He says and carry out what He means, and if that's evil, it's only to do good." Uttering the Faustian cry, "Now evil be my good" (*Creation*, pp. 387-88), he contends that only through his disobedience "was Eve made pregnant with mankind" (*Creation*, p. 399). He tells God early in the drama that "You've got to thin out the innocence down there" (*Creation*, p. 384) because without some opposite to innocence, some capacity for free will, there is no escape from stasis. "I am God's corrected symmetry," he asserts, "that festering embrace which keeps His whole world from impotent virtue" (*Creation*, p. 399). And God, too, confesses His ambivalence: "I have never before been in conflict with Myself" (*Creation*, p. 396). Even when God rejects Lucifer's plot to allow him to sit beside him in Heaven because "if God could love the Devil, then God has died," He asks, "Why do I miss him?" (*Creation*, p. 403). He needs his Lucifer as Faust needs his Mephistopholes.

But Miller implies that though Lucifer's disobedience frees humanity from "impotent virtue," it also poses a far greater threat, a world without moral distinctions and so without choice or responsibility. At the climax of the drama when he tries to stop Abel's sacrifice to God, Lucifer declares "one massive, eternal, continuous parole!/From here on out there is no sin or innocence/But only Man" (*Creation*, pp. 432-33). He offers the modern accommodation of good and evil, an easy neutrality that dissolves away any responsibility for action as well as guilt. In other words he attempts to reconstruct Eden, where "people would never come to hate themselves, and there's the end of guilt. Another Eden, and everybody innocent again" (*Creation*, p. 401).

Ironically, having failed to convince Cain not to murder Abel because "if man will not kill man, god is unnecessary" (*Creation*, p. 438), Lucifer accuses God of arranging Abel's murder. God admits that He did, hoping that Cain, remembering "his love for Abel and for me, even in his fury [, would] lay down his arms" (*Creation*, p. 441). He wanted Cain to *choose* good. Yet God discovers that "love . . . is not enough" and that human beings "love, and with love, kill brothers" (*Creation*, p. 444), a theme that runs through much of Miller's work. Even in this despair, though, Eve finds a basis of hope: "If [Cain] loved his brother, maybe now he feels . . ." (*Creation*, p. 443). Because humankind is born "not of dust alone, but dust and love," guilt and responsibility may emerge after innocence. "But what about Cain?" Eve asks. "How do I hand him his breakfast tomorrow? How do I call him to dinner? 'Come, mankiller, I have meat for thee?'" (*Creation*, pp. 442-43). And even as He disappears off the stage, God replies, "what did you say to me a moment ago--'Why can't we just live?' Why can't you do it? Take your unrepentant son and start living" (*Creation*, p. 443). As in Thorton Wilder's *Skin of Our Teeth*, Cain remains part of the human family, the agent of the ubiquitous potential for human violence.

Creation is highly untypical of Miller's work in its rather flat characterizations, quasimythical elements, and obscure dialogue. Its themes nonetheless appear in the rest of the canon, and the conclusion defines what he describes as the essential human predicament. Adam comments, "Cain, we are surrounded by the beasts! And God's not coming any more . . . Boy, we are all that's left responsible! (*Creation*, p. 446). It is in this world East of Eden that Miller's protagonists live, in a landscape without metaphysical certainties, where good and evil yet reside in the self and where choices must therefore be made and consequences borne.

Employing allusion to the Biblical narrative without the limitations of plot or character that make *Creation* such a contrived and often prosaic play, *After the Fall* directly embodies the crisis generated by self-knowledge. The protagonist, Quentin, recounts his story by repeating it to the Listener, who Miller says is Quentin himself, "turned at the edge of the abyss to look at his experience . . . innocent no more--to forever guard against his own complicity with Cain, and the world's" (*Theater Essays*, p. 257). Miller in effect presents three Quentins: a Quentin talking to the Listener, the Listener himself, and a Quentin reenacting his past, whom the narrator Quentin describes with frequent self-mockery. He serves as his own criminal, prosecuting attorney, and, in the guise of the Listener, jury; and what he reveals is a guilt that can render him incapable of risking life East of Eden in the waiting arms of Holga, his newfound lover. Once again paradox abounds: only acknowledgment of his evil can save him from spurious innocence, yet such truth can freeze the will.

Quentin recounts his inauthentic existence before the Fall--a "dinner table, and a wife, a child, and the world so wonderfully threatened by injustices I was born to correct. . . . Remember? When there were good people and bad people? And how easy it was to tell! . . . Like some kind of paradise. . . . Until I began to look at it."[18] When his friend Lou is called before the House Un-American Activities Committee and asks Quentin to defend him, Quentin is suddenly driven from his innocent garden--suddenly "nobody was innocent again," he comments, "And yet, we never were!" (*After the Fall*, p. 152).

Above all, Quentin must confront his own criminality. Even when Lou's wife, Elsie, tries to seduce him, he wonders, "No, no, it isn't only that Elsie tempted me, it's worse. If I see a sin why is it in some part mine?" (*After the Fall*, p. 157). Throughout, though he accuses others--his mother for the betrayal of his father, Louise for the failure of their marriage, Maggie for the violation of their love--he expresses a need "to somehow join the condemned in some way to start being real" (*After the Fall*, p. 180). He knows the blessings of his mother, his grateful client Felice, and Maggie to be fraudulent. He knows, too, that though he was seemingly noble in defending Lou he felt "joy" when Lou committed suicide because "my danger had spilled out on the subway tracks!" (*After the Fall*, p. 184). And even when he rightly accuses Louise of self-righteousness, demanding that she "say something, something important was [her] fault" (*After the Fall*, p. 169), he is "*dumbstruck*" to find himself before her "*clench fisted*" (*After the Fall*, p. 186) in the pose of a murdering Cain. And he reenacts his potential for violence with Maggie, squeezing her throat until she sinks to the floor out of breath. Indeed it is with Maggie that the criminality of his innocence explodes most fully. In their last encounter when she threatens suicide in order, Quentin, contends, to make him guilty, he admits that they had "loved each other's innocence as though to love enough what was not there would cover up what was." But, he goes on to say, there is an angel guarding the gate who reveals the truth of our fallen nature, "And no chemical can kill him, no blindness dark enough to make him lose his way; and you must love him, he keeps truth in the world" (*After the Fall*, p. 234). Despite his awareness that the barbituates Maggie has already swallowed are taking effect because her sighs signal the diaphragm being paralyzed, Quentin continues to argue with her, risking her life. "What can be so important to gamble her life to get?" he asks. He answers, "My innocence you see? To get that back you kill most easily" (*After the Fall*, p. 240).

The concentration camp tower which dominates the stage symbolizes the universal guilt that all share by dint of their common humanity. Quentin is struck that the stones "look so ordinary," wondering "Why do I feel an understanding with this slaughterhouse?" (*After the Fall*, p. 142). He then asks, "Why does something in this place touch my shoulders like an accomplice?" (*After the Fall*, p. 157). And at the end of the play, he comes to consummate self-knowledge:

> What love, what wave of pity will ever reach this knowledge--I know how to kill. . . . I know, I know. . . . Who can be innocent again on this mountain of skulls? I tell you what I know! My brothers died here. . . but my brothers built this place; our hearts have cut these stones! (*After the Fall*, p. 240)

At one point, standing at the foot of the tower, Quentin asks Holga if she ever feels some sort of "vague . . . complicity." She responds, ". . . no one they didn't kill can be innocent again" (*After the Fall*, p. 148). Though she was ignorant of the Holocaust, she does not protest innocence, accepting her share in the enterprise of evil--". . . I don't know how I could not have known" (*After the Fall*, p. 141), she laments. Miller comments in the "Foreword" that "Murder and violence require Innocence" (*Theater Essays*, p. 256). And Quentin bitterly cries, "Not to see one's own evil--there's power! And rightness too!" (*After the Fall*, p. 186). At last he passes judgment on himself: "I curse the whole high administration of false innocence! I declare it, I am not innocent!" (*After the Fall*, p. 210).

Confronting the beast in the mirror involves enormous risk. As Quentin remarks when Lou commits suicide, "Maybe it's not enough--to know yourself. Or maybe it is too much" (*After the Fall*, p. 184). At the end of the play, Quentin too arrives at self-knowledge, wondering whether to chance loving Holga after knowing that, to guard his innocence, he already has destroyed those who loved him. Holga offers hope in light of such debilitating awareness. She recounts her dream of an idiot child in her house--"and I bent to its broken face, and it was horrible . . . but I kissed it" (*After the Fall*, p. 149). When Quentin asks if it still haunts her dream, she confesses: "At times. But it somehow has the virtue now . . . of being mine. I think one must finally take one's life in one's arms, Quentin" (*After the Fall*, p. 148). As Quentin chooses to embrace life by opting to love again, he knows that Holga "hopes" precisely "because she knows," that hope emerges not in spite of but because of self-knowledge:

> To know, and even happily, that we meet unblessed. . . . And the wish to kill is never killed, but with some gift of courage one may look into its face when it appears, and with a stroke of love--as to an idiot in the house--forgive it; again and again . . . forever? (*After the Fall*, p. 241)

It is the temptation of innocence, not humanity's inherently criminal nature, that poses the most enduring threat to Miller's protagonists. At the very end of *After the Fall* when Quentin turns to leave the stage and confronts the several characters who have played roles in his life, he comes to

Felice, who twice "blessed" him for his apparent goodness to her. But when she is about to raise her hand in blessing again, *"he shakes her hand, aborting her enslavement"* (*After the Fall*, p. 242). His gesture captures a central theme in Miller's work, that nothing, nothing can enslave so insidiously as innocence--that the greatest of crimes is the self-ignorance that allows the tyranny of innocence to exist.

Notes

[1] Rollo May, *Love and Will* (New York: Norton, 1969), p. 165.

[2] Leonard Moss, "Biography and Literary Allusion in *After the Fall*," *Educational Theatre Journal*, 18 (1966), 40.

[3] Arthur Miller, "Introduction" *Arthur Miller's Collected Plays* (New York: Viking, 1957), I, p. 11. All further references to Miller's introduction will appear in the text.

[4] Arthur Miller, *The Price* in *Arthur Miller's Collected Plays* (New York: Viking, 1981), II, p. 329.

[5] Arthur Miller, *All My Sons* in *Arthur Miller's Collected Plays*, I, pp. 59, 58.

[6] Arthur Miller, *Death of a Salesman* in *Arthur Miller's Collected Plays*, I, pp. 132, 158, 160, 213. All further references to this work will appear in the text.

[7] Arthur Miller, *The Misfits* in *Arthur Miller's Collected Plays*, II, p. 121.

[8] Arthur Miller, *A Memory of Two Mondays* in *Arthur Miller's Collected Plays*, I, p. 358.

[9] Arthur Miller, as quoted in Phillip Gelb, "Morality and Modern Drama" in *The Theater Essays of Arthur Miller*, ed. Robert A. Martin (New York: Penguin, 1978), p. 211. All further references to Miller's remarks in his theater essays will appear in the text in the shortened form *Theater Essays*.

[10] Arthur Miller, *Timebends: A Life* (New York: Grove, 1987), p. 559. All further references to this work will appear in the text.

[11] Arthur Miller, *The Crucible* in *Arthur Miller's Collected Plays*, I, p. 311.

[12] Arthur Miller, *A View from the Bridge* in *Arthur Miller's Collected Plays*, I, p. 436.

[13] Arthur Miller, *Incident at Vichy* in *Arthur Miller's Collected Plays*, II, p. 288. All further references to this work will appear in the text.

[14] Arthur Miller, *Playing for Time* in *Arthur Miller's Collected Plays*, II, pp. 503-04. All further references to this work will appear in the text.

[15] Arthur Miller, *The Archbishop's Ceiling* in *The American Clock and The Archbishop's Ceiling: Two Plays* (New York: Grove, 1989), p. 39.

[16] Jack Kroll, "Theater," *Newsweek*, 11 December 1972, p. 71.

[17] Arthur Miller, *The Creation of the World and Other Business* in *Arthur Miller's Collected Plays*, II, p. 387. All further references to this work will appear in the text.

[18] Arthur Miller, *After the Fall* in *Arthur Miller's Collected Plays*, II, p. 149. All further references to this work will appear in the text.

Arthur Miller's *After the Fall:*
The Critical Context

Robert A. Martin

Two weeks after the premiere of *After the Fall* on January 23, 1964, *Life* magazine ran a special section of five pages with photographs and articles. The caption of the lead article read, "Marilyn's Ghost Takes the Stage."[1] In the following pages I would like to suggest that her ghost is still there.

But is *After the Fall*, as Robert Brustein has asserted, really a "breach of taste" and a confessional autobiography "of embarrassing explicitness"?[2] While it would be naive to claim that the play is without autobiographical elements, to what extent is it something that Brustein finds "embarrassing"? Embarrassing to whom? The audience, critics, author, or all three? It is very doubtful that Arthur Miller set out to embarrass anyone having had this play dancing in his head for so long. He, in fact, once mentioned to me that "I had two-thirds of that play written before her death."[3] Yet the accusation is leveled and persists that Miller thrust upon his audience something very wrong, "raw material," in fact, "in place of art."[4] And, as if this were not a strong enough accusation, the play has been further denigrated by being referred to as "tabloid gossip" and "a wretched piece of dramatic writing: shapeless, tedious, overwritten, and confused."[5] Something obviously has gone terribly wrong either with the man who wrote *After the Fall* or in the perceptions of many critics. Even *Life* magazine asked its readers: "Is it good taste?"[6]

The fault, however, if there is one, does not lie with Miller. The peculiarities in the staging of the play and the experimental form it employs are not blunders by the author or director, but quite natural progressions in the level of dramatic consciousness Miller has always asked of his audience. Further, the play is without ornamentation. It is bare, stark, and brutally to the point--a point that the audience is strongly encouraged to consider and to assimilate into its own experience. But the scarcity of details in the play apparently alarmed critics and audiences alike. There is no final resolution, no death for Quentin, and no easy answers that allow the audience to leave the theater feeling relieved in any way; in short--no catharsis. Unsettling for a society that seems to want quicker and easier solutions to all the difficulties of life. One critic has said that it is "unfortunate" that Miller tried in *After the Fall* to "reduce a multitude of differences to a single formula."[7] This is not "unfortunate." It is, on the contrary, the single most important aspect of the play, the very essence of Miller's attempt at a recognition--that is, that within us we have a common humanity. It is also apparent that in *After the Fall*, Miller did indeed, as Allan Lewis has observed, try "to expose his own anxiety as a revelation of mutual suffering with other men."[8] In doing so, curiously, the opposite effect was often and erroneously perceived.

Miller has said that "Each member of the audience is carrying with him what he thinks is an anxiety or a hope or a preoccupation which is his alone and isolates him from mankind."[9] Although some people may think they are unique in this way, Miller is adept at demonstrating his premise: that we do not always carry what is regarded as "his alone." There is a commonality in life that Miller sees society ignoring in favor of a much-touted and overrated individualism. To their credit, even the milder critics of the day were aware that Quentin "frequently addresses that audience directly, as if it were a friend."[10] But some critics also construed this narrative innovation as a distraction. What it actually represents, however, is Miller's attempt to lead the audience to a higher recognition--to the idea that, regardless of how different this staged experience may be, there is, nevertheless, an important connection between the play and the lives of everyone in the audience.

Elia Kazan recognized this connection early. In his director's notebook he probes deeply into the significance of the characters and action. Since Quentin is, of course, a rough equivalent to Miller, it is revealing what Kazan has to say: "Quentin (Miller, all of us) are in the habit of looking for the solution to our interior, intimate problems through something else: A woman, a cause, a religion."[11] But this is the formulaic mold that Miller and Kazan tried to break out of in *After the Fall*. For Miller, the major dramatic question in the play really is "What is there between people that is indestructible?"[12] What, when all the old patterns are obliterated, remains to save the individual from the edge of the abyss? What is there to combat the metaphorical concentration camps of our isolated minds and lives, the "human separateness and its ultimate consequence . . . organized abandonment."[13] Or, as Quentin asks rhetorically, "God, why is betrayal the only truth that sticks?" Kazan thought the answer could be found in the recognition "of our true natures--the truth of our behavior."[14] Psychologically intuitive, he suggests that the saving grace of mankind "is not some outside element like a philosophy . . . not 'others' . . . but confrontation of one's self, and RECOGNITION of one's true nature."[15]

It is difficult to believe that Miller approached the writing and staging of this play with an attitude very much different in his mind. He most certainly bares his own soul and history for all to see, and seriously examines this part of himself for perhaps the first time in his life. But this brings outrage. Miller has been attacked as a playwright, indeed even as a decent human being, for conducting a "vendetta against the former objects of his love."[16] Brustein also--with no small degree of pomposity--states that "the only new insight I was able to glean from these familiar episodes was that Mr. Miller must have talked his wife's ear off, since even in the act of viciously throttling her, he is explaining why she hates life, why she drinks, why she married him, and why she is trying to commit suicide."[17] "Familiar episodes," indeed; but to whom? What could Brustein possibly know about Marilyn Monroe to object so vehemently to Miller's portrayal of Maggie? Miller is obviously trying to be truthful, both to the play and to himself. "Looking back," Miller wrote in *Timebends*, "I could see that in disconnecting the fictional character [of Maggie] from any real person I was blinding myself to the obvious."[18] His original intention to have Quentin and Maggie merely part would, he later decided, be too easy, and "prevent the audience from disposing of the tale with comforting death" (*Timebends*, p. 527). Yet Maggie's death seems to evoke the very spectacle of ultimate disgust and poor taste in those critical of the play. Miller, twenty-five years later, saw that coming so quickly after Monroe's death, *After the Fall* "had to fail" (*Timebends*, p. 533). The reviews, he recalled, were mostly about a scandal rather than an art form: "with barely a mention of any theme, dramatic tension, or style, as though it were simply an attack on a dead woman" (*Timebends*, p. 534).

Critics and audiences alike were for some reason uncannily eager to jump on the anti-Miller bandwagon. "It seems to me," Miller has said, "an easy way out for people who will not or cannot examine the work at hand, so what they do is examine the author."[19] In their frenetic fervor to rescue and protect Maggie, critics and audiences were both conveniently avoiding the larger thematic implication of the play: that Maggie (or Marilyn Monroe for that matter) is essentially a dramatic personification dramatizing a process by which we come to understand and cope with conflict and chaos. Miller understands quite well that what critics are avoiding is their own denial of the play's larger meaning. The denial the critics engaged in while attacking Miller is, he has said, "the same kind of denial that has brought about the play's tragic ending" (*Timebends*, p. 534). This, too, is almost tragic; this, too, brings no catharsis, no insight. "If we want to describe life," Miller has commented, "we have to describe our own experiences . . . and what of it? The main thing is to reveal the meaning of all this and make a universal theme out of it, not a documentary feature."[20] The incredibly defensive posture of those who opposed the play often seems little more than an indictment of their own spectatorial attitude in which they exist in this world only passively. Miller thinks such people, most people in fact, "never got around to wondering why they are alive. They think maybe it is because they are breathing. . . . we live for something more than this, something we can only discover by baring our soul completely."[21]

Philip French, for example, in the *New Statesman*, curiously described Quentin as a lawyer, stalking "around the desk addressing a non-existent 'listener' and entertaining his family, friends, first two wives, and future wife."[22] Quentin may do a lot of unusual things, but to say that he is "entertaining" anyone is not only disingenuous, but completely misses the point of the play--that opposing forces of personality are constantly undergoing change and confrontation is great torment. What far too many critics have succumbed to, in a way they have rarely done before, is to place themselves critically and intellectually on the level occupied by the American public *in general* who as Miller has asserted, "do not play a part in the art works of our time. The working class is all but illiterate, the middle class is mostly sheep frightened of not liking what it should. . . . as a consequence [of this] narrowness of the audience, there is no body of peers worthy of [the playwright's] respect."[23]

It is rare in the history of the American theater that such critical outrage and anger has greeted a play and its author. One must wonder about the actual popular sentiment toward Marilyn Monroe in 1964. Had she already become a goddess, icon, or fantasy woman self-created and sustained by Hollywood film-makers? Miller claims there is no difference in a play's validity if the playwright appears in the play or not,[24] and cites Tolstoy and Crane as examples of authors whose work transcends their autobiographical elements. "We're flooded," Miller said, "with publicity and reportage in a way that is obvious no other civilization ever was. Between the television, and the movie magazines, and the newspapers, we've lost any respect for the imagination of man or any sense of what it means to synthesize experience."[25] Synthesizing experience in *After the Fall* means that Quentin must overcome the difficulty of self-recognition--that is, of coming to a reconciliation with himself that will make it possible for him to function on some sort of acceptable level in the future. And even though Quentin learns that he has spent his life trying, in different ways, to establish his innocence, the essence of his new-found recognition toward the end of the play is that, with reference to the concentration camp tower, "my brothers died here . . . but my brothers built this place."[26]

Those displeased with *After the Fall* seemed unable or unwilling to recognize the elements of existential and personal angst that Miller built into the play, thereby turning it into a public discussion of personal guilt and complicity. Self-realization is difficult; "mea culpa" even more so for American audiences, who prefer to leave their plays in the theater and the classroom. But perhaps Miller's scenario *is* flawed in that he overestimated the average theatergoer's and critic's intelligence, their basic powers of perception and introspection. There is obviously a defense mechanism in operation in the play that allows the audience to exonerate itself in the most direct and simple terms. It seems to have troubled critics greatly having not only to witness Miller's confession, but also to accept the format in which it is presented. The physical construction of the scenery, the spaces, the silences, and interplay between the actors also troubled viewers, who are traditionally more comfortable with a stage that possesses only furniture, and characters who totally reveal themselves without the necessity of thought or creative interpretation by the audience. Kazan, no novice in translating a playwright's theme and message to the stage, told scene designer Jo Mielziner that the stage itself should "seem primordial, as old as murder itself" and that "it should be cavernous, deep and dark . . . made up of the corners of his memory into which his mind has never penetrated before, because it never dared to."[27] But how daring is the average critic or audience, and how willing are they to strip away the layers of the past (like Peer Gynt peeling his onion) at the risk of finding little or nothing inside? Miller, however, had personally made that dramatic leap, and found in himself the courage and daring to put this play on the stage, even though "the people from Quentin's past are still very much alive,"[28] like those in Miller's own past, most of whom were in the audience on opening night. In his reassessment of the characters, Kazan concluded finally that Quentin "has given up the old 'answers' . . . he has come to question everything he used to NOT QUESTION."[29] To do that it took Quentin most of his life, and it took Miller, at the very least, all of the nine years prior to *After the Fall*. The similarity between what Quentin accomplishes in the play and what Miller was trying to accomplish now seems perfectly integrated. Like Quentin, Miller himself was "pursuing truth at whatever cost" and looking at his life in order to see "what really took place."[30] Quentin, however, has no theater full of people whom he must move to applause once each evening, nor does he have to face the same kind of critical fallout that Miller does whenever the play is produced.

It is interesting, perhaps laughable even, that critics have so fleeting an interest in looking even slightly beneath the autobiographical surface of the play. In seeking to universalize Quentin's experience Miller has somehow offended both the critics and his audience, and they have confused his motive as a process of merely shifting guilt onto themselves instead of seeing what the play really does, which is to show them a way out, a door they can pass through so they might stand reconciled with their past, like Quentin, like Miller, and have a clear choice in the future direction of their lives. Howard Taubman, one of the few perceptive critics of the play, recognized that *After the Fall* "seeks to understand, not to judge."[31]

At the core, however, of all the antagonism, anger, and opposition to the play, what remains, unfortunately, is that Miller's dramatization of his life with Marilyn Monroe has become ironically rewritten, twisted, and distorted, and the primary focus of the critics' denunciations. In trying to protect Monroe from Miller, they have instead darkened her name almost beyond repair. They tend to contradict themselves and are far too emotional about a woman they never met and never knew. For example, Richard Gilman wrote of "our preexisting feelings about Miss Monroe."[32] What does a theater critic know about her life that could possibly be more authentic than the memory and experience of her own husband? Are the "preexisting feelings" of a removed public reason enough to ignore the play's theme--that there resides in all of us somewhere the guilt and complicity with which we must come to terms? One possibility is that critics have failed themselves, their readers, and the play by focusing so stubbornly on the autobiographical elements to the point where they can discuss only the play's supposed incoherence and lack of shape, in spite of all the evidence that says otherwise.

Robert Whitehead has recalled that Miller phoned him only two months prior to opening rehearsals and told him "it just hit me that this play may be construed as a play about Marilyn."[33] Incredible? Yes, although altogether plausible. If Miller was indeed consciously set on examining the real Monroe specifically, and if he had an absolute commitment to bare his soul, the character of Maggie would certainly have been very different. Elia Kazan has recalled Monroe's infidelities to Miller with French actor, Yves Montand. "I saw the pain in [Miller's] face," said Kazan:

> Three years later, remembering the way he was that night, I knew there was more to the second act of *After the Fall* than he'd allowed himself to reveal. If he would dig into those bad times, to which I'd been an arm's length witness, if he'd go all the way and tell the truth of what Marilyn had done and what he'd felt, we might have a strong second act.[34]

So Miller was factually rather generous with Marilyn Monroe. He tells all he can tell without destroying parts of himself, and softens Monroe's character flaws greatly. And if Miller had been absolutely factually and completely truthful about Monroe, his critics would certainly have had a much more legitimate reason to criticize the play as being merely "about" her. Kazan, someone who should certainly know, also tells us that he "knew that there were scenes between her and Miller that were a lot more dramatic than those he'd let us see."[35]

It is somewhat incredible, though eminently human, that the same critics who took Monroe so lightly as an actress, and even mocked her while she was alive, were so utterly willing and eager to make her, as Kazan says, their "house martyr."[36] "They're all writing about her," Miller said in 1962 after her death, "and they can't because they don't know anything about her."[37]

After the Fall has become a play of audience misunderstanding, and represents a sad failure by critics to bridge the chasm which obviously exists in the moral and social fabric of contemporary society. Quentin has lost faith in the world and in himself, and is philosophically ill-at-ease with the context in which he finds himself. The major achievement for Miller, however, is that through an intensive introspection and recognition of his own complicity-guilt in the tragedies of others, he could bring the play to its fruition. "It requires," Miller has said, "everybody to do what I did, which is to stretch inwardly and outwardly toward an image larger than life."[38] Miller has decisively answered the larger question of the play, and perhaps its critics also, when he commented in an interview, "You ask why so many people bear a grudge against me: they resent it because I remind them that for thirty, forty, perhaps sixty years of their lives, they have never once stopped to wonder why they were alive. Well, I have stopped to wonder."[39]

Notes

[1]"Marilyn's Ghost Takes the Stage," *Life*, 7 February 1964, p. 64A.

[2]Robert Brustein, *Seasons of Discontent: Dramatic Opinions 1959-1965* (New York: Simon and Schuster, 1965), p. 243.

[3]Personal interview with Arthur Miller, March 1967.

[4]Richard Gilman, *Common and Uncommon Masks: Writings on Theatre 1961-1970* (New York: Random House, 1971), p. 152.

[5]Brustein, p. 244.

[6]"Marilyn's Ghost Takes the Stage," p. 64A.

[7]Edward Murray, *Arthur Miller: Dramatist* (New York: Ungar, 1967), p. 155.

[8]Allan Lewis, *American Plays and Playwrights of the Contemporary Theatre* (New York: Crown, 1970), p. 50.

[9]Lewis, p. 50.

[10]John McCarten, "Miller on Miller," *New Yorker*, 1 February 1964, p. 59.

[11]Nancy and Richard Meyer, "*After the Fall*: A View from the Director's Notebook" in *Theatre: An Annual of the Repertory Theater of Lincoln Center*, ed. Barry Hyams (New York: Hill and Wang, 1965), p. 67.

[12]Arthur Miller, as quoted in Olga Carlisle and Rose Styron, "Arthur Miller: An Interview" in *The Theater Essays of Arthur Miller*, ed. Robert A. Martin (New York: Viking, 1978), p. 289.

[13]Miller, as quoted by Carlisle and Styron, p. 289.

[14]Meyer and Meyer, p. 67.

[15]Meyer and Meyer, p. 67.

[16]Brustein, p. 246.

[17]Brustein, p. 246.

[18]Arthur Miller, *Timebends: A Life* (New York: Grove, 1987), p. 527. All references to this work will appear in the text.

[19]Robert A. Martin, "The Creative Experience of Arthur Miller: An Interview," *Educational Theatre Journal*, 21 (1969), 312; rpt. in *Conversations with Arthur Miller*, ed. Matthew C. Roudané (Jackson: University Press of Mississippi, 1987), pp. 177-86.

[20]Oriana Fallaci, "A Propos of *After the Fall*," *World Theatre*, 14 (January 1965), 79.

[21]Fallaci, p. 81.

[22]Philip French, "The Old Miller Stream," *New Statesman*, 10 November 1967, p. 651.

[23]Arthur Miller, "On Recognition," *Michigan Quarterly Review*, 2 (1963), 217; rpt. in *The Theater Essays of Arthur Miller*, pp. 237-51.

[24]Martin, p. 313.

[25]Martin, p. 314.

[26]Arthur Miller, *After the Fall* (New York: Viking, 1964), p. 127.

[27]Meyer and Meyer, pp. 46, 47.

[28]Meyer and Meyer, p. 48.

[29]Meyer and Meyer, p. 50.

[30]Meyer and Meyer, p. 51.

[31]Quoted in Dennis Welland, *Miller: The Playwright* (New York: Methuen, 1983), p. 94.

[32]Gilman, p. 155.

[33]Quoted in Richard I. Evans, *Psychology and Arthur Miller* (New York: Praeger, 1981), p. xi.

[34]Elia Kazan, *Elia Kazan: A Life* (New York: Knopf, 1988), p. 667.

[35]Kazan, p. 690.

[36]Kazan, p. 690.

[37]Benjamin Nelson, *Arthur Miller* (New York: McKay, 1970), p. 243.

[38]Arthur Miller, "Arthur Miller Ad-Libs on Elia Kazan," *Show*, January 1964, p. 97.

[39]Quoted by Fallaci, p. 81.

Watching the *Clock*

Gerald Weales

"A new play by Arthur Miller is not chopped liver." So Dan Sullivan wrote in the *Los Angeles Times* in 1979 (November 25) after going north to see the other theatrical Dan Sullivan direct a staged reading of *The American Clock* at the Seattle Repertory Theatre. Since it was a play in progress, the critic did not review it; he only recorded the occasion. He could not have realized how appropriate his gustatory metaphor was. *The American Clock* came close to being chopped liver before it reached its presumed final form. In his introduction to the version published by Grove Press with *The Archbishop's Ceiling* in *Two Plays* in 1989, Miller wrote, "I have no hesitation in saying that as it now stands, the work is simply as close to such a resolution as I am able to bring it" (p. xii). A dramatic resolution, that is, to "the Great Depression of the thirties."

In his *Times* piece, Sullivan reported that Miller had told a radio interviewer that the material for *Clock* had been "accumulating" since the 1960s. It had, in fact, been accumulating since the 1930s when Miller--like Lee Baum, his dramatic surrogate--was forced out of his comfortable nest into a world that was all sharp edges. Perhaps he meant that the material began to accumulate on paper in the 1960s. In that decade he began to look back at his family and what the Depression did to them in some of the fragments of *After the Fall* (1964) and more extensively in *The Price* (1968). Those two plays, however, dealt with protagonists' coming to terms with themselves in the present. Miller had something else in mind in *The American Clock*, an attempt to understand--or, at least, to present--a calamitous period in American history which--as Lee says in the opening speech to the 1982 *Clock*--was rivaled only by the Civil War in its impact on American society. In the *Two Plays* introduction, he wrote, "At bottom, quite simply, I wanted to try to show how it was and where we had come from" (p. xiv).

It was in the early 1970s that the writing began. Studs Terkel's *Hard Times* was published in 1970. Miller's first impulse was to adapt it as a play, but--as he told James Atlas in 1980 (*New York Times*, September 28)--"I soon realized that my own life was moving into it, until there was very little of Terkel left." Arthur A. Robertson comes from Terkel, as does most of the material involving the failed millionaires, and Louis Banks, who was in the pre-Broadway version and back again in the final one, makes a nice borrowed balance to Robertson, the black hobo alongside the money man as survivor. At least three people tell Terkel the story of the farmers' threat to lynch the judge, and a careful reading of *Hard Times* will turn up other incidents, allusions, characters who have been used and transformed by the playwright. Both the anecdotal material that Terkel presents and Miller's talent for sharp, contained scenes would appear to be compatible, but they work against one another--or so it seemed in the early stages in the making of the play. Ideally, the post-Crash scene in Broadway Tony's speakeasy should have the dramatic force of the one near the beginning of the play when the Baums, riding high in the 1920s, are introduced in a flood of cross-cut dialogue. Yet, the former is dependent on information-giving both within the scene and without--from Robertson and Lee, gray-wigged in the play's present time. It belongs to the larger picture--the "mural" as the play was called in 1980, the "mosaic" as Miller sometimes called it--in a way that the Baum scene, however exemplary, does not. "Difficulties with the play had to do almost totally with finding a balance between the epic elements and the intimate psychological lives of individuals and families like the Baums" (p. xiv), Miller said in *Two Plays*.

A University of Michigan press release in 1973 announced the production on campus of *The American Clock* in April, 1974, but when spring came *Clock* was withdrawn and replaced by *Up from Paradise*. *Clock* was still a work in progress five years later at Seattle Rep. Whatever Miller learned from the reading there, the play was presumably ready five months later when it was mounted, again under Daniel Sullivan's direction, at the Harold Clurman Theatre in New York. After a brief run it moved on to the Spoleto Festival in Charleston. The reviewers--by common consent, I suppose--did not cover the off-Broadway workout at the Clurman, but Spoleto was another matter. Frank Rich, then the new boy at the *New York Times* (May 27, 1980), praised the Baum family scenes and hoped that Miller would "cut away the clutter" before the play went on to New York. Get rid of Terkel, that is, and the "epic elements." T.E. Kalem in *Time* (June 9, 1980) had a similar reaction: "While the vignettes are interesting as social history, they diffuse attention." At Baltimore, on its way to Broadway, the play succumbed to the well-intentioned advice. Jack Garfein, the artistic director of the Clurman and one of the producers of the commercial venture, called for changes, which Daniel Sullivan opposed. Miller sided with Garfein and Sullivan was out, replaced by Vivian Matalon, who had just directed a well-received revival of *Brigadoon* (*Variety*, November 26, 1980, p. 127). In 1988 Miller blamed the Broadway failure on a bad production and, to quote interviewer Leslie Bennetts (*New York Times*, July 14), "his own capitulation to pressures to rewrite the material in ways that conformed to conventional expectations but robbed the work of its true voice." It is ironic that during the Baltimore run, he told the *Washington Post* (October 26, 1980) how happy he was to be back in the theater after working in films and television for here he had control of his own play. Some of the changes can be gleaned from the reviews--putting Rose and Moe in the speakeasy scene, adding a final glimpse of Moe with a nurse, discarding the farm auction scene and replacing it with Henry Taylor's telling about it when he turns up in Brooklyn. Despite the presumed improvements, *Clock* opened in New York to mostly unfavorable reviews and closed after twelve performances. Chopped liver.

The play did not die, for even badly reviewed Arthur Miller plays do not die. They tend to lie doggo until someone pumps life back into them. *The American Clock* did not have to wait long. It was published in 1982 by Dramatists Play Service (DPS), presumably restored to its earlier state--or some approximation of it; the DPS version has both the farm auction scene and Taylor in Brooklyn. It was issued in the same form by Methuen in 1983, after a production by the Birmingham Repertory Theatre. This version--the mural--is with us still; Methuen reissued it in *Plays: Three* in 1990, despite the intervening London success of Miller's major revision. Never happy with the early version, Miller reworked it in 1984 for a production at the Mark Taper Forum in Los Angeles, and it was this text, as he said in *Two Plays*, which Peter Wood "movingly and sometimes hilariously interpreted" (p. xii) at the National Theatre in 1986. When the National version was mounted at the Williamstown Theater Festival in the summer of 1988, Miller told Leslie Bennetts, "The spirit of the whole thing was far grayer on Broadway, but it was never intended that way; it was intended as a six-ring circus, which is what it is now. . . . Onstage it's a kind of vaudeville." The old subtitle, "A Mural for the Theatre," was replaced by "A Vaudeville" when *Clock* was published the next year in *Two Plays*.

Before I turn my attention to the vaudeville--which I saw and admired in London in 1986--let me consider the Baum family and their place in the play. Much was made in 1980 of the connection between the Baums and Miller's own family. Douglas Watt in the *New York Daily News* (November 21) began his review, "I wish Arthur Miller would write a play about his mother. He has made a stab at it in 'The American Clock.'" The tendency to see Rose Baum as Augusta Miller was heightened by the fact that she was played by Joan Copeland, Miller's sister, who came off better than the play did; she got a best-actress Drama Desk award for her performance. The press was titillated by the idea of Copeland's playing her own mother. Harold C. Schonberg went down to Baltimore to do a pre-opening article for the *New York Times* (November 16, 1980), and the result was a mildly amusing sibling-rivalry piece in which the playwright and his sister quarreled amiably about what their mother was like. Copeland was too young to know her as Miller did, the playwright insisted; Miller, being a male child, could not possibly understand her as Copeland did, the actress countered. Miller, of course, got the last word. "She's a character in a play," he said. "This is not her biography." There is a passage in *Timebends*, however, that indicates the degree to which Miller drew on his parents in creating Moe and Rose Baum. "Never complaining or even talking about his business problems, my father simply went more deeply silent, and his naps grew longer, and his mouth seemed to dry up," Miller said of his father's "failure to cope with his own fortune's collapse" (p. 112). He speaks of his mother's reaction to her husband as much as to the collapse itself: "her impatience at the beginning of the calamity and her alarm as it got worse, and finally a certain sneering contempt for him that filtered through her voice" (p. 112). The contempt is more obvious in the Rose of *After the Fall* than in the Rose of *Clock*, but the impatience that gives way to hysteria is clearly there. The Baums are Miller's family in the way that Lee is the playwright himself. Miller was fourteen when the Crash came and, like Lee, had to scramble for jobs, found the temporary comfort of a midwestern campus and made his way gingerly through a world in economic ruin.

Unless one is more interested in biography than in art or preoccupied with the way a writer's life feeds into his work, it is finally of minimal importance that the Millers became the Baums. Miller was right in the Schonberg interview; these *are* characters in a play. It is much more valuable to see how Miller uses the Baums than where they came from. He told an interviewer from the *New York Sunday News* (November 23, 1980), "I wanted the characters to represent *every* family touched by those times." In a sense, this is what the Kellers are in *All My Sons* and the Lomans in *Death of a Salesman*, but the Baums seem representative in a slightly different way, more like the Bergers in Clifford Odets's *Awake and Sing!* and the Gordons in his *Paradise Lost*. What they stand for is not simply a product of the dramatic action of which they are a part; they come to their play already wearing labels. Odets and Miller are such good playwrights and they have such sharp eyes for the details of family life that the characters escape from their ideational or thematic cages and take on a stage life of their own. The best of the Baum scenes for my money is not the one the reviewers seemed to like--the tearful moment in which an embarrassed Moe asks his son for a quarter--but the extended card-playing one in which the foolishness of the conversation joins the fear of eviction to push Rose over the edge.

There are two Baum plots in *The American Clock*. One involves Moe and Rose and their generation; the other belongs to Lee. The first chronicles the decline and fall of the Baums, which, like the decline and fall of the Gordons, is the account of a false paradise lost. The second is a typical story of a young man's leaving his family to find his way in the world--made atypical by the times. Both are necessary to the play, for it is an account of the collapse of society and of survival despite that collapse. In Lee's quest, he moves Left in the good 1930s tradition, but he remains too questioning to become Communist like the exasperated Edie in the aborted sex scene or the angry Irene in the relief office. Whatever Lee discovers about his society differs from the lessons learned by Ralph Berger or Leo Gordon. Odets's plays are part of the scene *The American Clock* depicts; they are both diagnosis and prescription and the audience is supposed to see the light. *The American Clock* is looking back at Lee's fumbling movement toward commitment, recording it, not embracing it. Whatever Miller's own commitment in the 1930s, he came to distrust Communist solutions. Lee's social education is important not for its details but as a reflection of individuals cut loose by events and forced to find new ways of coping in a society shed of its old certainties.

The difficulty for the first reviewers--if I may make a terrible Baum joke-- is that they could not see the forest for the trees. The Baums seemed to be recognizable figures in a recognizable family drama, somehow trapped in an animated history lesson. When Miller came to his final revision of the play, he had to make all the elements mesh. The Baums, who still have the lion's share of the action, had to be reduced to only one element within the total picture. If the mural would not do it, vaudeville would have to. Peter Wood, who I suspect is the begetter of many of the vaudeville elements in the 1989 published play, needed a text to work with.

After the long initial speeches of Lee and Robertson in the 1982 version of *Clock*, Robertson pulls off his gray wig and "*tosses it offstage*" to play his scene with the bootblack. In the 1989 version, Miller tosses that gray wig for good, brings Robertson and Lee permanently into the play's present, cuts much of their commentary, moves speeches around, gives some of their lines to other characters. For the most part, he sticks to the scenes of the earlier version, sometimes sharpening the lines, but he introduces new characters. The most important of these is Theodore K. Quinn who--as the introduction indicates--is based on a Connecticut neighbor of Miller's, a man who was for one day president of General Electric. An anti-monopoly capitalist, he serves--as Robertson does in a very different way--as a survivor of a catastrophe which destroyed more conventional businessmen. Miller continues to let his characters speak directly to the audience, comment on scenes and their significance, but the important thing is the way in which the performers are deployed. Whether it was Miller's or Peter Wood's idea, the performers remain on stage through the show. They step in and out of scenes and, when they are not playing a role, they become part of the chorus. This is true of the principals--Moe, Rose, Lee--as well as the actors who play multiple roles. When Rose and Moe make comments from the "*choral area*," they are both performers and characters; the device makes the Baums a part of the larger Depression picture as the actors playing them are members of the company. Their scenes are no longer uncomfortable realistic dramas embedded in a presentational context.

It is only a step from a speaking chorus to a singing one. Taking his cue from Rose and her piano, from those bridges in which the character, sometimes with her son and husband, sings snippets of the 1920s songs she loves, Peter Wood moved a jazz band on stage, introduced marathon dancers, added a host of songs from the 1920s and 1930s. The dramatic scenes continued to work as the minidramas they are--vaudeville sketches, now--but the play as a whole is--or ought to be--carried on the music and on the ensemble movement. The play opens with a baseball player tossing a ball from hand to hand as Quinn in the balcony begins to whistle and then to sing "Million-Dollar Baby" joined by the rest of the company. A very truncated version of Robertson's first speeches--shared among the company--opens the verbal play, and we move from scene to scene on the rhythm of popular music. Quinn is as much soft-shoe dancer as he is businessman, a Wood invention based on Miller's having told him, as he tells us in the introduction, that the real Quinn "was forever bragging about--and mocking--his mad love of soft-shoe dancing" (p. xix). There is even a new scene for Lee's cousin Sidney, who wants to be a song writer. He and Doris sing "Sittin' Around," ostensibly Sidney's work, but actually Miller's lyrics to music by Robert Lockhart, musical arranger for the production at the National. At the end, Lee and Rose begin to sing "Life Is Just a Bowl of Cherries" and the company joins in while Quinn and Robertson exchange possible explanations for the end of the Depression. "That's it!" Quinn says suddenly, bringing the discussion to an end. "God, how I love that music!" He begins to soft-shoe again and signals the audience to join the company in the song.

What are we to make of an ending like that? Leo Sauvage, in his review of the Broadway production in *New Leader* (December 29, 1980), described a final scene mentioned by none of the other reviewers: "the whole company sang of love in front of a projected image of the Statue of Liberty." That seems an odd finish for the play at that stage, but Sauvage's reaction to that scene, whether he saw or imagined it, embodies the dilemma that playgoers face with the later vaudeville version. He did not know whether it was "meant to convey a ray of hope, or provide a crowning sarcasm." Julia Pascal in *City Limits* (August 14, 1986) found the production at the National "soft":

"There is something obscene about making glossy entertainment about the suffering of the Depression; it should have an uncomfortable edge." *City Limits* is one of those London guides, like *Time Out*, which mix fierce opinions with useful information, but her remark raises the question about how sharp the edge has to be to cause discomfort. Back in 1980, faced with a less circusy show, Kevin Kelly (*Boston Globe*, November 27) chided Miller for making "the Depression seem like a holiday at Atlantic City." I find it hard to imagine that anyone singing "Life Is Just a Bowl of Cherries," even at the best of times, accepts the lyrics as truth, or that the musical finish of *Clock* erases the pain implicit in the Depression scenes. Productions may differ. According to Leslie Bennetts, during the singing of "Cherries" at the end of the Williamstown production, a voice broke through and asked, "Could it happen again?" The published play has no such line, nor does it need one. There is ambiguity enough in the final scene to allow the playgoer to ask that question for himself. Sauvage's reaction quoted above posits an either-or, "a ray of hope" or "a crowning sarcasm." Why can't it be both? Why can't the singing of "Life Is Just a Bowl of Cherries" be both satirical and positive? "In her own crazy way she was so much like the country," Lee says of Rose at the end of the play. "There was nothing she believed that she didn't also believe the opposite."

There is nothing doubtful about Miller's positive intentions in *The American Clock*. The play is not simply a chronicle of disaster, but an account of our coming through. In the final speech of the 1982 version, Robertson says that, whether or not it was Roosevelt's intention, "the people came to believe that the country actually belonged to them. . . . that belief is what saved the United States." Quinn is given those lines in the 1989 version. In the 1930s, the initial despair following the Crash gave way to strained optimism. "The only thing we have to fear is fear itself," Roosevelt said at his first inaugural. In *Just Around the Corner* (1967), "A Highly Selective History of the Thirties," Robert Bendiner quotes the famous opening of *A Tale of Two Cities* ("it was the spring of hope, it was the winter of despair") and adapts it to his own purposes:

> so much has been written of the wintry despair of the Thirties, of lives stunted and people demoralized, that its springtime hopefulness has been underplayed. Admittedly one would be more fatuous than Pollyanna herself to talk about the good old days when fifteen million people were unemployed, but there is no harm--indeed there is some use--in recalling the fact that in those same years much of the dross of American life was stripped away, truths were faced with more candor than is normally in evidence, and America came closer to knowing its aims and its real worth than at any time before or since.

This is an eloquent variation of what Arthur Miller is saying in *The American Clock*.

Just as important as the political and economic solutions, workable and unworkable, that marked the 1930s, was a spirit that informed the decade, one that can best be seen in the popular culture of the period. Take the movies, for instance. Film scholars have come to recognize that the comedies and musicals of the 1930s were not so much escapism for a sorely tried populace as a reflection of an American energy that was central to our recovery. That energy is a necessary ingredient in Miller's mural-mosaic-vaudeville, and it is the music that provides the beat. No wonder that the play ends not with Quinn's "belief" line but with his declaration of love for the music. The ticking of the American clock may have indicated that time was running out for some people and some attitudes; the Twenties, whatever the Gershwin song says, were not here to stay. Yet, the fun and frivolity of that period did not disappear. It was tempered in hardship and reemerged as a tough-tender quality for which the best label can be found in Lee Baum's last words about his mother: "all I know for sure is that whenever I think of her, I always end up--with this headful of life!"

Temporality, Consciousness, and Transcendence in *Danger: Memory!*

Steven R. Centola

According to Arthur Miller, every individual plays some part in the imaginative invention of the attributes of the Other: "much of each of us is imagined by the other," he tells us; "we create one another even as we actually speak and actually touch."[1] Inherent in such a constructivist perspective is a Sartrean emphasis on the primacy of consciousness. As in earlier plays like *Death of a Salesman* and *After the Fall*, where almost every scene is filtered through one person's interior consciousness, the dramas in *Danger: Memory!--I Can't Remember Anything* and *Clara*--once again track the movement of the mind and show its power to shape reality and define the identity of the self.

In *I Can't Remember Anything* and *Clara*, Miller specifically explores the effect of memory on one's perception of reality and understanding of the self. Certain circumstances--a casual dinner engagement with a close friend in *I Can't Remember Anything* and the murder of a man's daughter in *Clara*--revive in the main characters crucial memories that, when examined, raise serious questions about not only the characters' past choices and values, but also the meaning of their lives. Burdened with either guilt or despair, these characters attempt to escape responsibility for their lives through denial or self-delusion. The bad faith that is evident in such escapist behavior becomes the basis for powerful dramatic action in these plays. Commenting on his characters' bad faith, Miller writes: *I Can't Remember Anything* and *Clara* are

> about trying not to remember, about the tactics people consciously take to forget pain. Some things make one feel the agonies of guilt and other things you find yourself bearing. In "I Can't Remember Anything," a woman uses the

absence of memory as a defiance and in "Clara," a man is prevented from remembering by his own culpability.[2]

Miller skillfully renders the workings of a person's interior consciousness in these plays by showing how the mind first denies but eventually can be made to accept significant meanings associated with resurrected memories. This process is embodied in his plays' epiphanic movement. Coinciding with the external action is an internal movement toward revelation. As the outer action progresses, the characters in both plays become increasingly more self-conscious, and eventually experience what Miller describes as "a kind of imploding of time--moments when a buried layer of experience suddenly surges upward to become the new surface of one's attention and flashes news from below."[3] In *Clara*, in particular, this implosion is very powerfully presented as the logical culmination of a series of intensely personal probes and painful disclosures. Miller skillfully blends music, screen images, and lighting in this play to externalize his central character's inner conflict and to exhibit the movement in psychic time that leads gradually to the final cathartic revelation.

I Can't Remember Anything is lighter in tone and mood than *Clara* and is developed in a more straightforward realistic fashion. Set in the present "*in a nondescript little wooden house on a country back road*,"[4] *I Can't Remember Anything* is similar to *Incident at Vichy*, *The Price*, and *The Archbishop's Ceiling* in that it also exhibits many of the characteristics that Jean-Paul Sartre associates with the theater of situations. There are few props, hardly any exists or entrances, and only two characters passionately defending their contrasting perspectives of life and death.[5] The plot is simple but engaging. Two elderly friends dining together discuss their conflicting views of the past and the meaning of their restored memories. At first, they hold almost diametrically opposed views, but as the play progresses, they stake common ground in the joyous remembrance of shared friendships with deceased loved ones. As a result of her encounter with Leo, Leonora learns that there is meaning in the life she has lived and that realization, perhaps, is enough to help her face her own mortality.

When the play begins, it is clear that Leonora is not coping well with the aging process. Upon entering Leo's house, she almost immediately pours herself some bourbon, a practice that has become part of her regular routine and has evidently only served to exacerbate the problems that have resulted from her aging. Leo indicates as much when, after sarcastically commenting on her drinking habits, he wryly observes that she has once again wrecked a new car. But instead of admitting her guilt, Leonora reacts defensively and blames her accidents on the position of the light poles. Miller, of course, uses Leo's sarcasm in this scene to reveal her culpability and inability to face honestly her problems.

It soon becomes evident that Leonora's problems are more serious than the humorous treatment may at first seem to indicate. Leonora suffers from severe depression and tells Leo that she wishes she had died; she complains that life has no purpose and describes herself as totally useless (*ICRA*, p. 8). Miller paints a portrait of despair in this characterization of Leonora. She is a woman who has lost all hope and finds no meaning in life. She is particularly disgusted by the "greed and mendacity and narrow-minded ignorance" (*ICRA*, p. 24) that she believes is ruining America. It would be easy to link such social criticism to her despair and suggest that her disillusionment with America has soured her on life, but it may be more accurate to suggest that her despondence colors her perspective of everything else and even causes her to view America as a society in decline. However one defines the chain of causation leading to her depression, one thing is certain: Leonora suffers terribly from angst and tortures herself with the feeling that life has no meaning.

Because she views everything as meaningless, she particularly sees no reason for remembering the past or assigning any significance to memories of her life. The past is as unreal to her as a story about someone else she has read in a book. That impression, in essence, becomes her excuse for failing to remember. Since she views her own life as unreal, she assumes that it must also follow that no one else would be too much concerned about whether or not she has existed. For this reason, when Leo admonishes her for forgetting the memories of beautiful experiences from her past, she responds by asking: "What earthly difference does it make?" For Leo, the difference is obvious and significant: "it's not a book, it's your life," he pointedly reminds Leonora (*ICRA*, p. 14). Leo hates to see Leonora living in bad faith and hurting herself by attempting to deny her life and responsibility for it.

Leo clearly lives in good faith. He has no illusions about life but still refuses to abandon hope. Although he is an atheist and has a realistic understanding of the innumerable problems confronting contemporary society, he does not view life as meaningless. In fact, he insists on doing his part to give it meaning. He tells Leonora that he wants his organs donated to the Yale-New Haven Hospital when he dies, and he assists a friend by checking his mathematical calculations for the new bridge in town. Leo recognizes that each person is responsible for the meaning he derives from life's experiences. He knows that meaning only exists if a person creates it. His life has been meaningful because he has made it so with his altruistic behavior.

Leo, therefore, is not afraid to accept his past. In fact, he relishes special memories about close friends and the joyous occasions they once shared together. He recalls past scenes with such remarkable detail that he helps stimulate Leonora's memory by recreating the past for her. By reviving these memories and engaging in impure reflection to review their acts and the meanings assigned to them, Leo enables Leonora to come to terms with her life. She gradually comes to see the beauty in her life that she has either forgotten or failed to recognize, and eventually reaches a point of acceptance, what Sartre calls a "liberating instant"[6]--a point where she freely chooses to start anew to face life's challenges and her own mortality.

Leonora's acceptance is very nicely conveyed in her sensual dance with Leo. As she dances, she abandons her defenses and inhibitions; in his stage directions, Miller describes her movement by saying she "*lets herself into the dance fully*" (*ICRA*, p. 27). Later, she proves that she has made some progress that evening by not forgetting to call Leo once she returns home. Leonora seems to understand that there is no reason for being depressed over not finding some purpose in life. Like the beauty of nature that surrounds her and that she so greatly admires, life simply is. Like Leo, she perhaps learns to accept the fact of existence and not question *why* she lives. With Leo's guidance, she may even come to understand what is real: her life (including the memories of the past), death, and the freedom to act responsibly toward others. Only through acceptance of these facts of life can Leonora find the meaning that she so desperately wants to attach to her existence.

As the play ends, one can only hope that Leonora will eventually learn from Leo's example that meaning can reside in every act if one recognizes in it its inherent value and relevance to other people. Unlike Leonora, whose only communication with her son is the occasional record he sends her from Sri Lanka, Leo stays vitally connected to others through his responsible behavior. He will even remain part of other people's lives long after he dies because of his donation of his organs for scientific research.

In Leo, Miller seems to have created a model of human conduct--a person who faces life's absurdities (aging and death, most noticeably) with courage and the determination not to be defeated in his struggle to give it meaning. Leo lives a noble existence and even takes the necessary steps to ensure that his death will also be meaningful. From Leo, Leonora (and the audience, for that matter) learns that, even though the human condition is fundamentally absurd, life can be endowed with meaning if a person accepts the freedom and responsibility to make the most of it.

A similar view is found in the companion piece to *I Can't Remember Anything*, *Clara*--a work that also has much in common with Sartre's theater of situations. Like *I Can't Remember Anything*, *Clara* has a small cast, can be played with very few stage properties, and is unified around a single plot that depicts the curious conflict that arises when two men with notably different outlooks on life are brought together to unravel a murder mystery. As in Sartre's theater of situations, the action in Miller's play seems designed primarily to set in opposition the conflicting values and perspectives of the central characters. Their opposing views represent the counterforces that are in perpetual conflict, the universal opposition, says Miller, of "the voice of realism and the flesh against the immortal spirit that transcends gain and loss; the death-in-life, and the life-in-death" (*Timebends*, p. 591).

At first glance, *Clara* seems to follow the conventional pattern of a murder mystery. A detective, Lew Fine, has arrived at the scene of a brutal murder and tries to solve the crime by piecing together a series of fragmentary clues extracted from the victim's father, Albert Kroll. As Detective Fine proceeds to interrogate Kroll to get leads for his case, Kroll is thrust back to scenes from his past that both indict him for his involvement in his daughter's death and lead to the disclosure of facts essential to solving the crime. While both men are eager to capture the man who murdered Clara Kroll, their search for clues leads them into direct confrontation over their past choices of opposing value systems. The challenge Fine poses to Kroll is particularly significant because it clearly shows that Miller structures his drama not merely to solve the murder mystery, but also to show how the pattern of stage movement involving the criminal investigation coincides with Kroll's slow progression toward self-realization and acceptance of his culpability and responsibility. Through several key revelations, Kroll reaches a moment of intense crisis and decision--a moment when he must decide whether to accept his life and values or reject his past choices as meaningless. Kroll's decision is painful and poignant, and it produces the kind of heightened self-awareness typically associated with tragedy.

Clara takes place in "*a small lighted area*" surrounded by darkness.[7] When the play begins, Kroll is lying unconscious on the floor of his daughter's apartment. He has probably fainted from the severe shock of seeing his daughter's savagely mutilated body. Once he becomes conscious of his situation, Kroll has difficulty following Fine's line of questioning and occasionally remarks that everything seems "unreal" to him (*Clara*, p. 40). With his suggestive lighting and emphasis on the effect of such a shock on Kroll, Miller indicates that the major conflict in the play is occurring within the mind of Kroll, who can no longer clearly distinguish between reality and illusion. His dissociated psychological state soon becomes evident as Kroll intermittently reenacts conversations from the past with Clara; living in his mind, the memory of Clara takes on an imagined reality that has such force that she actually appears to be present before him. Even though she is dead, she still remains as real in his mind as she appeared when she was alive. Moreover, the smile of love on her face, frequently referred to in the stage directions, indicates that the love between them transcends the experience of death too. Certainly, Kroll's love for Clara is not in itself a problem, but his refusal to accept her death is an act of denial that suggests he wishes to take refuge in the past and escape from his present reality.

It does not take Fine long to figure out that Kroll's forgetfulness and digressive stories indicate his unwillingness to reveal something that could be useful to the police in their investigation. Kroll suffers from mental blocks because of his guilt. As Kroll periodically drifts into reveries of the past and talks as if Clara were present, Fine warns him: "What you can't chase you'd better face or it'll start chasing you. . ." (*Clara*, p. 37). It is ironic, though, that while Kroll's momentary lapses may be designed to avoid direct confrontation with the reality of his daughter's death, those key reenactments of scenes from his past are what bring him to full conscious awareness of his guilt and chosen values.

As in *Death of a Salesman* and *After the Fall*, in *Clara* Miller very skillfully weaves together the past and the present action to convey the hidden logic of causation which propels the action toward its inevitable climax. After Kroll relives scenes with his daughter that define his value system, he then must face the challenge to those values that Detective Fine presents. This slow back and forth movement coincides with a progressive heightening of the dramatic tension as Kroll becomes increasingly conscious of the tremendous influence he exerted on the development of Clara's value system.

At first in horror, and eventually with great pride, Kroll admits that his commitment to human rights and social equality was firmly and deeply instilled in his daughter--a fact dramatically demonstrated by his moving remembrance of young Clara asking him to tell the story of the time he saved his black troops from a lynching party in the South. As he finishes his story and remembers receiving a kiss from his proud daughter, he sees clearly his complicity in her death. Her admiration of her father and respect for his values led her to work first in the Peace Corps and then later in prisoner rehabilitation--a career that unfortunately involved her in a romance with the convicted murderer who ultimately would kill her. As this painful revelation occurs in the harrowing climactic scene, Kroll must decide whether to embrace or reject his values. As Miller indicates, Kroll chooses to embrace his life, even though doing so necessitates accepting the tragedy of Clara's sacrifice:

> He had lived a decent life, even a courageous one, with a certain instinct for being useful to others. He was what Whitman might have thought of as one of his "Democratic men." But in the past twenty years Kroll has changed, become like others. . . . But in this bloodied room where his daughter died he is confronted with that ideal again. Must he disown it, suffer guilt and remorse for having misled his child? Or, despite everything, confirm the validity of the ideal and his former trust in mankind, in effect   keeping faith with the best in himself, accepting the tragedy of her sacrifice to what he once again sees was

and is worth everything? The play ends on his affirmation; in her catastrophe he has rediscovered himself and glimpsed the tragic collapse of values that he finally cannot bring himself to renounce. (*Timebends*, pp. 590-91)

Like Leo in *I Can't Remember Anything*, Kroll realizes that life is not perfect, but he also knows that fact does not excuse the individual from attempting to live by a code of honor that gives meaning to human existence. Like Proctor in *The Crucible*, Von Berg in *Incident at Vichy*, Quentin in *After the Fall*, and so many of Miller's other characters, Kroll knows that he alone must choose his path to personal salvation. He can face life's absurdities without illusions and nobly struggle to bring justice into the world through his actions, or he can deny his freedom and flee from his responsibility. In perhaps the most painful of situations, Kroll refuses to abandon hope and chooses to believe in human possibilities. He transcends his daughter's tragedy by transforming his guilt into social responsibility.

Like the rest of Miller's drama, the plays in *Danger: Memory!* explore the tragic dimensions of human existence while affirming the possibility for individual transcendence of the debilitating forces that pose a constant threat to the survival of humanity. Whether he is investigating the crippling effect of guilt and self-delusion in *Clara*, or examining the extent to which the absence of memory can conveniently distort the reality present in remembrances of the past--as happens in both *Clara* and *I Can't Remember Anything*, Miller, in this late stage of his career, clearly reveals his continued interest in the phenomena of temporality, consciousness, and transcendence. Because of the strong emphasis he attaches to the ethical implications of such ontological concerns, Miller leaves his audience with no uncertainty about his enduring allegiance to a moral code that stresses both self-determinism and social responsibility. For even while demonstrating the awesome power of illusion and self-delusion, these plays, like his earlier drama, suggest that choices exist which enable the individual to attempt to live an authentic existence. In *Danger: Memory!*, the choices his characters face are real and the possibilities inherent in such choices are considerable.

Notes

[1]Author's Note to *Two-Way Mirror: A Double-Bill of Elegy for a Lady and Some Kind of Love Story* (London: Methuen, 1984), n.p.

[2]Miller, as quoted in Mel Gussow, "Arthur Miller: Stirred by Memory," *New York Times*, 1 February 1987, Sec. 2, p. 30.

[3]Miller, *Timebends* (New York: Grove, 1987), p. 590. All further references to this work will appear in the text.

[4]Miller, *I Can't Remember Anything* in *Danger: Memory!* (New York: Grove, 1987), p. 3. All further references to this play will appear in the text in the abbreviated form *ICRA*.

[5]Jean-Paul Sartre, "Forgers of Myth" in *Sartre on Theater*, trans. Frank Jellinek (1946; rpt. New York: Pantheon, 1976), p. 41.

[6]Sartre, *Being and Nothingness*, trans. Hazel E. Barnes (1956; rpt. New York: Pocket, 1966), p. 612.

[7]Miller, *Clara* in *Danger: Memory!*, p. 33. All further references to this play will appear in the text.

Scripting the Closing Scene:
Arthur Miller's
The Ride Down Mount Morgan

June Schlueter

In the Afterword to the Methuen edition of *The Archbishop's Ceiling*, Christopher Bigsby calls that play, along with *Some Kind of Love Story* and *Elegy for a Lady*, "a major new phase in the career of America's leading playwright." He hastens to add, "but the break is not as radical as it may appear"; Arthur Miller's earlier plays, though governed by social and political concerns, were also a prelude to the later plays' fascination with "the problematic status of the real."[1]

Miller's play, *The Ride Down Mount Morgan* (1991) continues and nuances that fascination as it explores the appetites and the anxieties of a writer turned insurance executive who for nearly ten years has been married to two women. As Gerald Nachman, writing for the *San Francisco Chronicle*, notices, "In this memory (dream?) play, it's hard to tell if [Lyman Felt] is living a fantasy, having a delusion, is in a coma or has died and is reassessing his life as he watches it play out."[2] Surely the socially engaged playwright of the 1940s and 1950s is still apparent in this work, which may be read as a document of the moral narcissism of the Reagan years or, conversely, as a questioning of monogamy as the prevailing marital structure of the Western world. But this textual amalgam of past, present, future, and imagined events, in which the contours of the real are difficult to define, invites us into a psychic and artistic space that seems especially intriguing to the maturing Miller.

The Ride Down Mount Morgan, which opened in London in October 1991 after some ten years in the writing, features a lying and lionized figure of a man, Lyman Felt, whose romantic hunger and lust for life have, he believes, entitled him to a double share. In New York, he lives on the upper east side with Theo, a woman of intelligence, fashion, and restraint, his wife of thirty years and mother of their grown daughter. In Elmira, he lives with Leah, a sexy businesswoman twenty-four years his junior, whom he married nine years earlier, shortly after their son was born. In theory and practice, the arrangement works. Lyman shuttles between the two cities with energy and ease, taking pleasure not only in his own masterful orchestration of two distinct and complementary wives and lives (one Lyman drives racing cars, the other stays within the speed limit) but also in the variety and challenge: the effect of two wives is rejuvenating. Moreover, in marrying the two women he loved, Lyman, unlike colleagues who have one wife and a bevy of mistresses, is being honest. Or so Lyman would have himself believe. The challenge to his life is a challenge of his own making: stranded atop Mount Morgan on a snowy day, Lyman removes the barrier from the icy road and hazards all. The ensuing car crash lands him in hospital, where both wives are summoned to his side.

Lyman's decision to try the hill despite its dangers signals the end of the stable, if unconventional, drama of his double life and the beginning of the dangling clause of self-examination that was intended to bring closure to his play. Lyman admits to Leah that he had reached the point of feeling that "it had all died in me . . . ," that "this whole ten-year commute was just . . . ludicrous!":

> I thought if I walked in two-three in the morning out of a roaring blizzard like that . . . you'd be so amazed, you'd believe how I needed you . . . *and I would believe it too!*[3]

But he does not admit that the ride down the icy Mount Morgan road may have been suicidal. "You must face it, Lyman," says his lawyer friend Tom, "you moved that barrier . . . ," upon which Lyman protests, "That was not suicide--I am not a cop-out!" "Why," Tom asks, "is it a cop-out to have a conscience?" (*Mount Morgan*, pp. 82-83). Himself a Quaker who is honest with his clients and faithful to his wife, Tom hopes it was such an attempt, for, as Theo reads his hope, "It would indicate a moral conscience" (*Mount Morgan*, 39). But for Lyman, who has tyrannized and colonized others in the name of a private vision of honesty, admitting that he got back in the car not "to stop the dying," as he told Leah, but to die, would be agreeing to the judgment that he fears others would have of him if they knew of his bigamy: in short, that "all I am is shit" (*Mount Morgan*, p. 85).

Nine years earlier, Lyman, on safari in Africa with Theo and their daughter, Bessie, had challenged a lion, shouting--roaring--his defiance of monogomy and his love of his life until the kindred beast turned back: "I don't sacrifice one precious day to things I don't believe in--and that includes monogamy, yes, we love our lives, you goddam lion!" (*Mount Morgan*, p. 61). For Lyman, wide-eyed and exhilarated, the moment was an epiphany: "His roar hit my teeth like voltage and suddenly, it was so clear that . . . I've always been happy with you, Theo!--I'm a happy man and I am never going to apologize for it again!" (*Mount Morgan*, p. 62). For an audience with knowledge of the lion's power over life and death on the plains, its extravagant mating habits, and its uncontested virility,[4] the identification between lion and Lyman is secure. But just as the lion's "enormous echoing roar" becomes a "relaxed guttural growling" (*Mount Morgan*, 61) so does this King of Human Beasts, the model of rampant sexuality, become deenergized. And with the diminishing of exhilaration and uncompromised happiness comes the guilt he had lost on the plains.

Moral conscience, of course, has always been a concern of Miller, whom a *New Republic* critic once called "America's connoisseur of guilt,"[5] and in this play, Miller escorts us into that dangerous and powerful space where the psychic and the artistic converge. Lyman's ride down Mount Morgan and its afterhours in the hospital may be read as the need of a man who has left his sexual signature on the world to justify and monumentalize himself. His fictional hero, whose life he has tried to lead, is an insatiably hungry man who has embraced life honestly and energetically, provided happiness to two women and two children, and, in the end, is guilt-free. The real Lyman Felt, however, is desperate and confused; he careens off the icy road, narrowly escaping death and forcing the dreaded but wished for showdown with the two wives, whose meeting will provide the occasion--and the necessity--for judgment and resolution.

That meeting, in fact, as dramatized in the first act of *Mount Morgan*, is Lyman's imagined version of a meeting that is about to take place--and does take place--offstage. Alone in the hospital room, Lyman anticipates the encounter: "My God, how could I have done this!--Christ, I can just see them! . . . Oh how terrible! It can't happen, it mustn't happen" (*Mount Morgan*, p. 4). Nonetheless, the "*catastrophic vision*," as Miller's stage direction describes it, appears: "Oh, I can just see it . . . Bessie is weeping, oh poor darling! But not Theo . . . No, Theo is completely controlled, yes . . . controlled and strong . . ." (*Mount Morgan*, p. 4). Ellipses mark the halting tones of one who is witnessing an encounter just coming into focus or of a writer himself about to script the scene. Slipping out of his cast to meet the dramatized vision, Lyman at first looks on in "*high tension*" (*Mount Morgan*, p. 4), then finds himself relaxing in approval. Wife No. 1 offers comfort and commentary; she is handling herself with aplomb. But then Wife No. 2 appears. Clapping his hands over his eyes, the twice-married man pleads with whatever or whomever is shaping the vision: "No, she mustn't! It can't happen! It mustn't!" (*Mount Morgan*, p. 6). But it does:

> Leah. My husband; he cracked up the car on Mount Morgan. You?
> Bessie. My father. It was a car, too.

> Lyman. O dear God, not this way . . . please! . . . if I could only get myself
> over to the window . . . and out! (*Mount Morgan*, p. 7)

But the conversation between the two wives is going well. Lyman approves: "What admirable women! What strong, definite characters." He assumes authorial control of those characters, wondering, "Now what would they say next?" (*Mount Morgan*, p. 8). The recognition scene, clearly under Lyman's own control, follows:

> Theo. Who *are* you?
> Leah. I'm Leah. Leah Felt.
> Theo. . . . Felt!
> Leah. Lyman is my husband.
> Theo. Who *are* you? . . . --Who the hell *are* you!
> Leah. I'm Lyman's wife. (*Mount Morgan*, p. 10)

Just before the scene ends in a blackout, Theo, historically a monument of strength, collapses. Later, when Lyman learns from Tom that the two women have indeed met, he tests the accuracy of the encounter he had imagined: "Theo . . . didn't collapse, did she?" (*Mount Morgan*, p. 25)--and learns that she did.

The present moment of the play, the document of actual, imagined, and remembered events in the hours following the crash, owes its existence to Lyman's sudden and desperate feeling that his life, which "could never stand still for death," now needs others'--and his own--approval. For "by a certain age," he realizes, "you've got to stand there nobly and serene . . . and let death run his tape out your arms and around your belly and up your crotch until he's got you fitted for that last black suit" (*Mount Morgan*, p. 68). Lyman, at fifty-seven, is approaching that age.

Tellingly, his father, who died at fifty-seven, is a recurring figure in Lyman's mental landscape, an admirable, critical, and fearful ghost, who stalks his son with a broad black cloth. The Albanian immigrant appears in the second part of Lyman's initial vision, cruelly reproaching his son for general failure and beginning to register an attitude toward women that resonates in Lyman's memory:

> Never talk business with women, God only makes them for one thing, obey
> God. Your teeth stick out, ears stick out, everything stickin' out, I'm sorry to
> say you very stupid boy, big disappointment. (*Mount Morgan*, p. 2)

Later in the act, he directs his young son to "Stay off the roof--very bad for business the way you fucking all these girls up there"--and includes his wife among his disappointments: "Stupid woman. I thought a Jewish woman gonna be smart. You both a big disappointment to me" (*Mount Morgan*, p. 24). When Father reappears in Act II, still critical of Lyman's behavior, his provoked son urinates in his Panama hat, then begs forgiveness. Near the end of the play, Father makes his final appearance in the theatre of Lyman's mind, at the very moment when Leah refuses to allow their son, Benjamin, to see him. Terrified, Lyman thrashes and shouts from beneath the billowing black cloth that Father has cast over him, eventually succeeding in flinging it off.

For Lyman, Father is an insistent reminder of his own mortality, despite an "anachronistic energy" (*Mount Morgan*, p. 68) that seduces him into wanting to believe he need never yield. So also is Father, who praised Muslim polygamy, contributing author of Lyman's troubled (arguably abusive) relationships with women, whom he consistently characterized as sexual objects--"God only makes them for one thing" (*Mount Morgan*, p. 2), "All whores, these American girls" (*Mount Morgan*, p. 47). Yet despite the patches of dialogue that recur in Lyman's stubborn dramatizations of this intimidating man, the son admires "how connected he was to his life; couldn't wait to open the store every morning and happily count the olives, rearrange the pickle barrels. People like that knew the main thing." But Lyman doesn't: "What's the main thing, do you know?" (*Mount Morgan*, p. 19). If Lyman fought fiercely for anything in his life, it was for his son, born nine years earlier. When he learned of Leah's pregnancy, he pleaded with her not to have an abortion: "I've already named him . . . His name is Benjamin after my mother's father who I loved a lot, and Alexander after my father" (*Mount Morgan*, p. 20). To persuade her to bear the child, he promises marriage, then marvels "Why are we so *connected*?--Do you feel it?" (*Mount Morgan*, p. 63).

Connectedness, demeaning sexuality, and death: Father represents all these to Lyman, who attempts to reconcile his feelings for his father even as this presence from the past threatens to neutralize Lyman's high-minded reading of his life and claim him for the grave.

Coincidentally, at the time of the ride down Mount Morgan, Lyman is not only approaching the age of his father's death; he is also approaching the ten-year mark in his double marriage. When he wooed Leah, he tried to tempt her into commitment by noticing the difference in their ages: "when you're thirty-six I'll be sixty . . . Dummy, you're not listening; when you're forty-six I'll be *seventy*" (*Mount Morgan*, pp. 21-22). At the time, Leah is twenty-three, which means that when Lyman is fifty-seven, the present in the play, she is thirty-three. Tellingly, their Faustian bargain was for ten years:

> Lyman. I thought if we lived together let's say ten years, you'd still be in the
>   prime, and pretty rich, and I'd . . .
> Leah. . . . Walk away into the sunset?

> Lyman. I'm trying to be as cruelly realistic as life, darling. (*Mount Morgan*, p. 22)

But Lyman cannot walk away into the sunset without a reprise of his life--and without a final judgment. Hence he spends his hospital time attempting to present and to justify the self he has performed. Imagining the closing scene, the man who at twenty had sold poems to the *New Yorker* and a short story to *Harper's* and who had admitted to Leah that "The only reality to me is still poetry, the words" (*Mount Morgan*, p. 14) once again turns author, this time in a final effort to inscribe himself.

Miller's strategy is to provide multiple perspectives on the marital partners, including each wife's retrospective of events. Hence Leah, narratively or within dramatized scenes, presents the first year of her relationship with Lyman, leading to their September marriage in Elmira: a conversation in the park following their initial sexual encounter; Lyman's impassioned plea that she not end the pregnancy; their visit to New York, when Lyman made love to both Theo and Leah in one evening; the birth of Benjamin; their July trip to Reno, when Lyman claimed to have torn up the papers divorcing him from Theo. Theo, too, participates in shaping the story: she speaks of an early moment of closeness when, as college students, they skinny-dipped in the river; she dramatizes a later close call with a shark at Montauk and participates again in the thrilling African safari.

The question throughout the play is whether these are the women's perceptions or Lyman's, whether the boundaries separating each memorial event are merely the transitions of his mind in various states of awakening and drug-induced dream. Both women appear to offer their judgments of the other, Theo, for example, saying of Leah, "She's exactly the type who forgets to wash out her panties" (*Mount Morgan*, p. 28), and Leah, speaking of Theo, telling Lyman, "your hatred for that woman is monumental" (*Mount Morgan*, p. 70). But these perceptions sound suspiciously like Lyman's own and may well be perceptions within perceptions, crafted by an omniscient, omnipotent author preparing to script the closing scene.

The challenge to Lyman is to close the text of his double marriage in a way that will vindicate his unorthodox behavior and leave him guilt-free. In one obviously hallucinatory scenario, the two wives in aprons each stand atop a staircase on either side of him, planning menus of his favorite meals, then descend to kneel at his bedside and suck his fingers. Leah and Theo lie on Lyman's bed as Lyman "*stretches out over both of them*": "Oh what pleasure, what intensity! Your counter currents are like bare live wires!" (*Mount Morgan*, p. 29). But in another, which may, in fact, be reality, Lyman's cry that he is not a monster becomes prelude to an "explosion of grief" (*Mount Morgan*, p. 82) in which all three--and Bessie--weep. In the final moments of Miller's play, Theo breaks down, appearing without a skirt and insisting, "I can say 'fuck,' you know" (*Mount Morgan*, p. 80); admitting her mistreatment of Lyman, she wants only to take care of him at home. Yet moments later, with Lyman insisting he gave her "the good life" (*Mount Morgan*, p. 81) and pleading "You can't really leave me, Theo---you can't!" (*Mount Morgan*, p. 88), the wife of thirty years leaves. Leah, too, who earlier accused Lyman of not knowing right from wrong, departs, saying she would try to stop by the next day but refusing to bring Benny along. Lyman defends himself mightily, claiming he has given Leah nine years of happiness and saved her from "lonely post-coital showerbaths" and "pointless pillow talk" (*Mount Morgan*, p. 81). As she gestures to leave, Lyman, "*with a scared laugh*," cries, "You all pulling out?--What is this?" (*Mount Morgan*, p. 83), uncomprehending and unrepentant despite earlier tears.

Contrasting sharply with the earlier version/vision of doting domestics waiting on his several appetites, this final scene leaves Lyman alone and unshrived. Fighting off an intruding father, he begs Leah to listen, for now he understands why he drove down the mountain; he understands that he had started to die. Confessing he no longer felt the quickening excitement of the New York/Elmira commute, he realizes that no one, not even Bessie, is willing to defend him. After his daughter's simple homily--"There are other people"--Lyman, as playwright and as revisionary moralist, admits he is paralyzed. Unable to write the moral ending the women prefer, he cannot script the closing scene, for "in some miserable dark corner of my soul I'm still not sure why I'm condemned." "Are you hearing me? Are you in this room!" (*Mount Morgan*, p. 86), he cries, and we wonder whether they were.

Perhaps more explicitly than any of Miller's plays, *The Ride Down Mount Morgan* insists upon the elusiveness of the real, presenting an unfinished portrait of a life needing verification but trapped within the shifting boundaries and orthodox marital morality of Miller's play. As William A. Henry III notices in *Time*, "The chief revelations occur in flashback, and the play's hallucinatory nature makes them all a little suspect."[6] Indeed, were it not for the presence of Nurse Hogan, who anchors the present in the hospital room, it would be easy to be seduced into questioning even the basic circumstance of the play. One might even wonder whether Lyman was still atop Mount Morgan, trying to decide whether to remove the barrier or not and imagining the scenario that would follow if he did. But the Nurse, who has no prior claim to a place in Lyman's imagination, lends palpability to his bandages and cast, compelling signs that the car crash has occurred. And Miller ends the play with Lyman, having failed to script the closing scene of his double life, in conversation with the Nurse, a warm, black "piece of the sun" (*Mount Morgan*, p. 87), who refuses to judge him. Nurse Hogan tells of ice fishing with her husband and son and of a conversation in the cold about used shoes. Struck by the simplicity and the beauty of that dull but decent family bond, Lyman marvels "What a miracle everything is!" (*Mount Morgan*, p. 88) and weeps.

Notes

[1] Christopher Bigsby, "Afterword" to *The Archbishop's Ceiling* by Arthur Miller (London: Methuen, 1977), p. 93.

[2] Gerald Nachman, "An American View of the London Stage," *San Francisco Chronicle*, 30 December 1991, p. E2.

[3] Arthur Miller, *The Ride Down Mount Morgan* (London: Methuen, 1991), p. 85. All further references to this work will appear in the text.

[4] See John Sparks, *The Sexual Connection: Mating the Wild Way* (London: Sphere, 1979), pp. 23-24.

[5] Matt Wolf, "*The Ride Down Mount Morgan*," *Plays & Players*, (December 1991/ January 1992), p. 30.

[6] William A. Henry, III, "Arthur Miller, Old Hat at Home, Is a London Hit," *Time*, 11 November 1991, pp. 100-01.

Index

Chinese people, 62, 63
City Limits, 132, 133
Civil War, 127
Claudius, 33
Clytemnestra, 20
Cobb, Lee J., 19, 31, 66
Cohn, Ruby, 38, 41
Colossians, 89
Comedie Francaise, 38
comedy, 27, 28
Connecticut, 12, 131
Conversations with Arthur Miller, 49, 67, 73, 76, 106, 126
Copeland, Joan, 129, 130
Corinthians, 89
Crane, Stephen, 122
Czechoslovakia, 59

Dance of Death, The, (Strindberg), 59
Danube, The (Fornes), 34
Darwin, Charles, 62
deconstructionist criticism, 24
DeMann, Paul, 24
didascalia, 13, 32-40
Dolan, Jill, 71, 72, 76
Doll's House, A, (Ibsen), 19
Drama Desk Award, 129
Dramatists Play Service, 38, 40, 129
Dunnock, Mildred, 31

Eastern Europe, 22
Eden, 110, 112, 113, 114
Edison, Thomas, 62
Ellison, Ralph, 105, 107
Elmira, 143, 148, 149
Emperor Jones, The, (O'Neill), 59
Endgame (Beckett), 38
England, 23
Ephesians, 89
Esslin, Martin, 14, 78, 79, 81, 82, 84, 85
Estragon (*Waiting for Godot*), 81
Europe, 12, 22, 24
European audiences, 13
European playwrights, 22
European people, 13
existential drama, 78
existentialism, 78
experimental theater, 19
expressionism, 59
expressionistic lighting, 61
expressionistic setting, 60

expressionistic technique, 13, 60

Fall, The, (Camus), 102
Faulkner, William, 22, 23
Faust, 113
Feminism and Theater, 69, 76
feminist criticism, 14, 24, 69-75
Feminist Rereadings of Modern American Drama, 76
Finn, Huck, 64
Fitzgerald, F. Scott, 23
Florida, 54
Ford, Henry, 22
Fornes, Maria Irene, 34
Fox, George, 92
Franklin, Benjamin, 62
French, Philip, 122, 126
French audiences, 22
French drama, 29

Garfein, Jack, 128
General Electric, 131
German drama, 29
German expressionists, 66
Gershwin, George, 134
Gilman, Richard, 124, 125, 126
Glaspell, Susan, 34
Glass Menagerie, The, (Williams), 35, 40
Goodrich, B. F., 62
Gordon, Leo (*Paradise Lost*), 131
Gordons (*Paradise Lost*), 130, 131
Great Britain, 12, 22, 23, 24
Great Depression, the, 22, 44, 48, 66, 127, 130, 132, 133
Greek drama, 24, 29
Greek tragedians, 66, 103
Greene, Graham, 112
Grove Press, 127
Gynt, Peer, 123

Hairy Ape, The, (O'Neill), 59
Hard Times (Terkel), 127, 128
Harold Clurman Theatre, 128
Harper's, 148
Harris, Rosemary, 20
Harry Crowe Ransom Humanities Research Center, 49, 57
Harvard Guide to American History, 23
Harvard University, 18, 88
Hayman, Ronald, 84
Henry III, William A., 149, 150